MOSQUITOS OF WORLD WAR 2

AIRCRAFT OF THE ACES: MEN & LEGENDS 14

MOSQUITOS OF WORLD WAR 2

OSPREY AVIATION

del Prado publishers

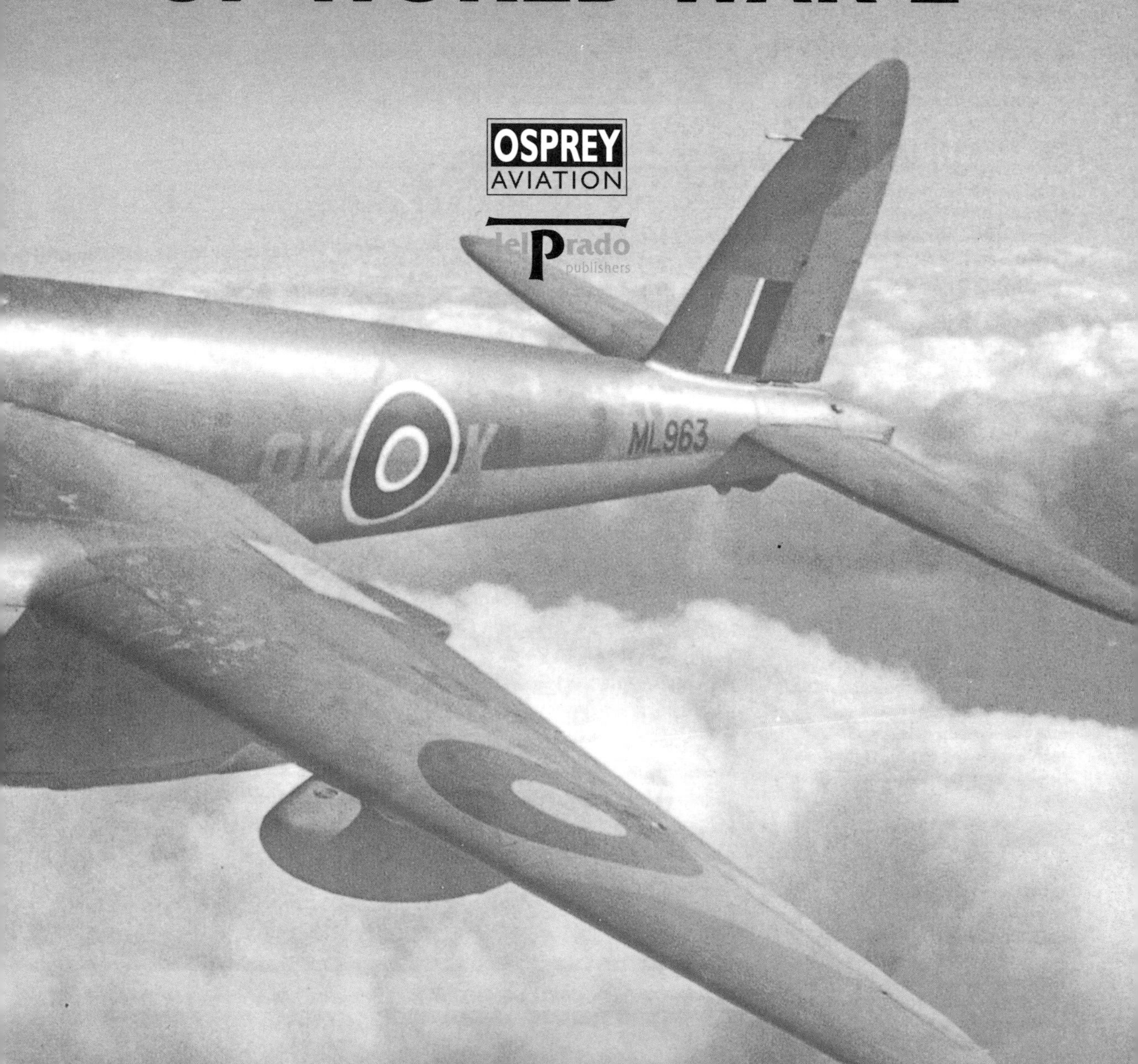

Front Cover
On 11 April 1944 six Mosquito FB VIs of No 613 'City of Manchester' Sqn performed one of the most accurate low-level bombing raids of the war against the Dutch Central Population Registry, housed in the Kunstzaal Kleizkamp Art Gallery close to the Peace Palace. The registry had become a prime target following its use by the Gestapo to hold records pertaining to Dutch families deemed suitable for deportation to concentration camps, or for reprisal executions of the relatives of resistance fighters. The following description of the raid was printed in Leslie Hunt's volume Twenty-One Squadrons (Garnstone Press, 1972);

'On 11th April, flying at only 50 ft, Wg Cdr Bateson led six Mosquitos, the plan being for three pairs to come in at two-minute intervals dropping high-explosives and incendiary bombs. Bateson led the first pair in, skimming house tops, making straight for the target building. A German sentry on duty at the front door screamed with horror as he threw away his rifle and ran for his life. Flt Lt P C Cobley, in the second plane, saw his leader's bombs going "right in the front door". A parade was in progress in the yard behind the building and some off-duty soldiers were playing football. No further goals were scored as Cobley's aircraft scattered troops in all directions with more bombs, right on target. Sqn Ldr Newman led in the next pair. The house was now partly obscured by smoke but he and his colleague dropped incendiaries across it. Last in were Flt Lt V A Hester and a Dutch pilot. Hester attacked with incendiaries and delayed-action high-explosives but the Dutchman's bombs hung up. Despite two more circuits and runs over the target he could not release them and had to return home without scoring a hit.'

Having reduced the five-storey building to rubble without causing any damage to surrounding structures, the Mosquitos returned to Swanton Morley, in Norfolk. A first-hand account of the raid, entitled 'The House in the Hague', was given by Wg Cdr Bateson on BBC radio on 1 May 1944, and three days later participating crews were presented to His Majesty King George VI.
(Cover artwork by Iain Wyllie)

Publisher: Juan María Martínez
Editor-in-Chief: Juan Ramón Azaola
Based on: Mosquito Bomber/Fighter Units 1942-45

Text by Martin Bowman
Cover Artwork by Iain Wyllie
Aircraft Profiles by Chris Davey
Figure Artwork by Mike Chappell
Scale Drawings by Arthur Bentley

DISTRIBUTION:
I.S.B.N (for the whole work): 84-8372-207-0
I.S.B.N (for this volume): 84-8372-342-5

COMAG Magazine Marketing
Tavistock Road
West Drayton
Middlesex
UB7 7QE
Telephone number: 0870 7297999
Subscriptions and back numbers :
WOODGATE
Aircraft of the Aces Subscription Offer
Freepost TN 7153
PO Box 95
Hastings
TN35 4BZ
Telephone number: 01424 755577
The price of each part is £ 4.95
(with the exception of No 1 at £ 1.95).

AUSTRALIA
Distribution: GORDON AND GOTCH LIMITED
Subscriptions: WELDON by mail
Reply paid 1900
Aircraft of the Aces Subscriptions
P.O. Box 1900
Mona Vale NSW 1658
Telephone number: (02) 9979 0222
Fax number: (02) 9979 7107
Back issues: These can be ordered through your newsagent, or write to Aircraft of the Aces, Gordon and Gotch Limited, PO Box 290, Burwood, Victoria 3125. Please enclose cover price plus A$ 1.50 p&h per issue.

NEW ZEALAND
Distribution: GORDON AND GOTCH (NZ) LIMITED
Subscriptions: WELDON by mail
Freepost 108466
Aircraft of the Aces Subscriptions
P.O. Box 47863
Ponsonby, Auckland 1034
Telephone number: (09) 377 3798
Fax number: (61 2) 9979 7107
Back issues:
Gordon and Gotch (NZ) limited
PO BOX 24013, Royal Oak, Auckland, New Zealand

SOUTH AFRICA
Distribution: RNA
Subscriptions and back orders:
JACKLIN ENTERPRISES
Private Bag,12
Centurion,0046
Tel.: 011 652 1897
Fax.: 011 314 2984
Subscriptions Email Address:
Subscribe@jacklin.co.za

CONTENTS

LOW-LEVEL RAIDERS

In November 1941, Blenheim-equipped No 105 Sqn of No 2 Group at Swanton Morley airfield, in Norfolk, became the first unit in RAF Bomber Command to receive the revolutionary new de Havilland B Mk IV Mosquito. Although the bomber/photo-reconnaissance (PR) prototype (W4050) had flown on 25 November 1940, the only versions in service by 1941 were those used for PR work. Production had only begun at all after a long, and sometimes painful, development phase, and at one stage the project had almost been abandoned altogether. At Hatfield, de Havilland management knew that their two-crew, unarmed, wooden bomber design, which relied on speed alone to out-distance enemy fighters, was a winner, even before it had left the drawing board. However, in London at this time unarmed bombers were an anathema. When de Havilland finally received a contract for 150 Mosquitoes on 30 December 1940 it was not specified how many would be fighters and how many would be photo-reconnaissance versions, let alone bombers.

In June 1941 the fighter version was approved. Convincing the Air Ministry that they should also order into production an unarmed, wooden, bomber version was only achieved the following month after

On 15 November 1941 de Havilland Chief Test Pilot, Geoffrey de Havilland Jr, demonstrated prototype Mosquito W4064 to Wg Cdr Peter H A Simmons DFC, OC No 105 Sqn, and his air- and groundcrews at their Swanton Morley base. That same month the first Mk IVs came off the Hatfield production lines, and on 17 November W4066 became the premier Mosquito B Mk IV bomber to enter RAF service when it was received by Simmons' unit – No 105 Sqn's first operation took place on 31 May 1942. B Mk IVs were initially so scarce that No 105 Sqn often had to share aircraft with its sister-squadron, No 139, in order to perform operations from its Norfolk base

Aircrews from both Nos 105 and 139 Sqns pose beside a B Mk IV at RAF Marham. At far left (with his back to the camera) is Jamaican-born Flg Off Pereira of No 139 Sqn, seen here talking to Flt Lt J Gordon (unfastening his 'Mae West'). No 139 Sqn flew their first operation on 2 July 1942 when two B Mk IVs carried out a high level bombing raid on Flensburg

strong lobbying by de Havilland, but especially when the Mosquito was seen to perform exactly as the company said it would. In trials in December 1940, the prototype, which was fitted with Merlin 21 engines with two-speed, single-stage, superchargers, had reached speeds of 255 mph. On 16 January 1941 W4050 outpaced a Spitfire in tests at 6000 ft, and in July the aircraft (this time fitted with Merlin 61s) reached 433 mph at 28,500 ft!

When the Air Ministry finally gave the go ahead for the bomber variant, it ordered some 50 aircraft, each capable of carrying four 250-lb bombs, and further specified that the last 10 aircraft out of the 19 PR Mosquitoes contracted should also be completed as unarmed bombers. These aircraft retained the short nacelles of the early models, and came to be known as the B IV Series I. W4072, the prototype B IV bomber, flew for the first time on 8 September 1941. The 292 B IV Series II bombers that followed (27 were later converted into PR Mk IVs) differed in having longer nacelles, and they could also carry two 50-gallon droppable wing tanks in addition to a 2000-lb bomb load – made possible by simply shortening the tail stabiliser of each bomb.

On 15 November 1941 No 105 Sqn's OC, Wg Cdr P H A Simmons DFC, and his crews were greatly impressed when de Havilland Chief Test Pilot, Geoffrey de Havilland Jr, arrived over the airfield in W4064. The 'wooden wonder' was far removed from the Blenheim both in power and performance, and Geoffrey de Havilland treated the unit to a spectacular piece of flying, racing low across the grass airfield at 500 ft at a speed in the region of 300 mph. The Hatfield test pilot then put the Mosquito into a vertical bank at about 3000 ft, before pulling into a tight circle that produced vapour trails from the wing tips. Only the air gunners failed to be impressed, as they were now surplus to requirements on the Mosquito, while the navigators would have to learn to operate the radio.

On 17 November W4066 – the first Mosquito bomber to enter RAF service – was received at Swanton Morley by the AOC No 2 Group, AVM d'Albiac, and his staff. A further three Mk IVs (W4064, W4068 andW4071) were later delivered by Geoffrey de Havilland and Pat Fillingham. In December No 105 Sqn moved to Horsham St Faith, just outside Norwich. Deliveries of the new aircraft were slow because of the need to develop the shortened-vane 500-lb bomb, which would then allow the Mosquito to carry four 500 'pounders' in place of the smaller 250-lb bombs. By mid-May 1942 just eight Mk.IVs were operational, one of which was fitted with Lorenz beam approach equipment, while another (DK286) boasted the new Mk XIV bomb sight for operational testing.

No 2 Group were eager to despatch Mosquitoes on operations as soon as possible, and the de Havilland bomber duly made its combat debut at dawn on 31 May 1942 in the wake of the RAF's first ever 'Thousand Bomber' raid – the latter had attacked Cologne. Four Mk IVs (the first of which was piloted by Sqn Ldr A R Oakeshott DFC), armed with 500-lb bombs and F.24 cameras, took off from St Faith and dropped their ordnance on the recently devastated city. They then quickly photographed the results of Operation *Millenium* before returning to base. Oakeshott was the first to reach the target area, overflying Cologne at 24,000 ft and dropping his four bombs from this height. However, smoke from the 'Thousand Bomber' raid had by this time settled at 14,000 ft, thus obstructing the squadron leader's photo run. Oakeshott duly returned to Norfolk, but two other Mosquitoes (flown by Plt Offs W D Kennard and E R Johnson) were downed by anti-aircraft fire over the target area.

Just after noon on the following day two crews (Plt Off Costello-Bowen and Wt Off Tommy Broom, and Flt Lt J E Houlston and Flt Sgt J L Armitage) again bombed Cologne from high level, although on this occasion they both returned safely. Later that afternoon Sqn Ldr R J Channer DFC took off and flew in thick cloud to within 60 miles of the city before diving down at almost 380 mph to low level to take more photographs. On the evening of 1 June two more Mosquito B Mk IVs sortied to Cologne but one failed to return.

The Mosquitoes at Horsham St Faith repeated the same tactics on the second and third 'Thousand Bomber' raids – the second was flown against Essen on 1/2 June, and the third and final raid targeted Bremen on 25/26 June. Flt Lt D A 'George' Parry and Flg Off Victor Robson flew

No 105 Sqn B IVs DZ353/E and DZ367/J formate for the camera at altitude. The latter Mosquito failed to return from a raid to Berlin on 30 January 1943, Sqn Ldr D F W Darling DFC and Flg Off W Wright both losing their lives. DZ353 later served with No 139 Sqn before joining No 627 Sqn, No 8 Group (PFF), as AZ-T on 24 November 1943. On 8 January 1944 it crashed whilst taking off from the Vickers-Armstrong factory at Weybridge following a double gear leg collapse – neither its pilot, Wg Cdr G H B Hutchinson, or navigator, Flg Off F French, were seriously injured. Subsquently repaired and re-coded AZ-B, the veteran bomber was shot down during a raid on the marshalling yards at Rennes on 8 June 1944, with the loss of Flt Lt H 'Harry' Steere DFM and Flg Off K W 'Windy' Gale DFC, RAAF. The former was actually a Spitfire ace from 1940, having served with No 19 Sqn

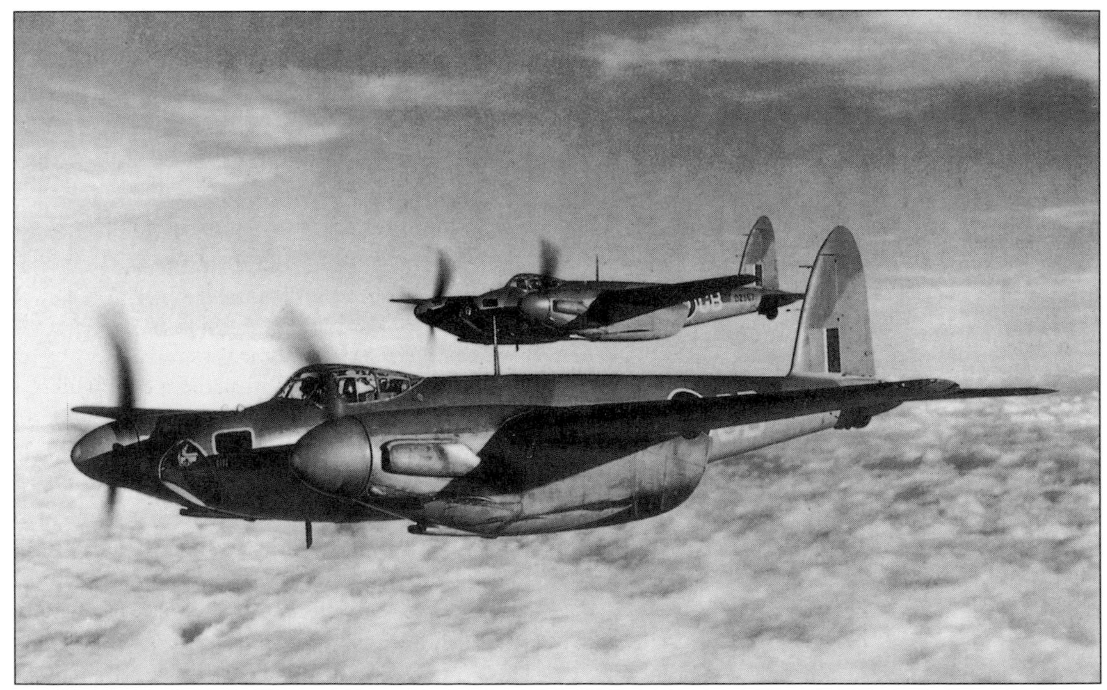

Wg Cdr Hughie Idwal Edwards was born in Mosman Park, Western Australia, to Welsh parents on 1 August 1914. Although he was just 28 years of age when he took command of No 105 Sqn for a second time in August 1942, he had already won the British Empire's highest military medal, the Victoria Cross, for his leadership of nine No 105 Sqn Blenheim IVs during Operation *Wreckage* – a daring daylight bombing raid on Bremen on 4 July 1941. His receipt of the VC made him only the second Australian aviator to receive such an award (the first had been presented to Lt F H McNamara of the AFC during World War 1). On 10 February 1943 Edwards was promoted to temporary group captain and made Station Commander of RAF Binbrook. By 1944 he had taken up an appointment in South East Asia Command, holding a Senior Air Staff Officer rank until the end of 1945. Edwards was awarded the OBE in 1947, and in 1958 he was promoted to air commodore, before retiring from the RAF in 1963. He then returned to his native country and became Governor of West Australia in 1974 – he was knighted during his period in office. Sadly, he was only able to fill this job for nine months before failing health forced his premature retirement. Air Commodore Sir Hughie Idwal Edwards VC, KCMG, CB, DSO, OBE, DFC*, KStJ – Australia's most decorated airman – died on 5 August 1982

a lone 2 hr 5 min round trip to Essen and dropped their four 500-lb bombs on the target, but smoke again rendered photography impossible. On 25/26 June six No 105 Sqn B Mk IVs flew bombing and photo-recce missions both during and after the third 'Thousand Bomber' raid. These first sorties helped gain experience for the operations that lay ahead.

No 139 Sqn was formed at Horsham St Faith on 8 June. Headed by Wg Cdr Peter Shand DFC, the unit was manned by crews and a handful of Mosquito Mk IVs from No 105 Sqn. On 2 July the first joint attack took place when four aircraft from No 105 Sqn carried out a low-level attack on the U-boat yards at Flensburg whilst two Mosquitoes from No 139 Sqn bombed the same target from high level. Two Mosquitoes were destroyed by German fighters, with Gp Capt J C MacDonald being made a PoW and the recently-promoted Wg Cdr A R Oakeshott DFC being killed, along with his navigator Flg Off V F E Treherne DFM. Sqn Ldr Jack Houlston came off the yards pursued by three Fw 190s, whilst Flt Lt G P Hughes was chased by two more after being hit by flak. Both pilots made good their escape by hugging the wave tops and using +12 lbs of boost, which allowed them to outpace their pursuers.

On 11 July six Mosquitoes from No 105 Sqn bombed the Flensburg yards once again as part of a diversion for 44 Lancasters sent to hit the U-boat yards at Danzig. Plt Off Laston returned with part of his fin blown away by flak, while Flt Lt G P Hughes and Flg Off T A Gabe were killed when their Mosquito crashed possibly as a result of flying too low. Sgt Peter W R Rowland was somewhat luckier, however, as he returned to Horsham with pieces of chimney pot lodged in the nose of in DK296!

The rest of July saw a mixture of daylight operations ranging from low and high level bombing using cloud cover against targets at Ijmuiden, in Holland, and cities throughout Germany. The primary purpose of these raids was to cause the air raid sirens to sound, which resulted in maximum disruption to German industry.

THE EDWARDS ERA

On 3 August 1942 Wg Cdr Hughie I Edwards VC, DFC arrived from Malta to take over command of No 105 Sqn. An Australian who had won the VC for his courageous leadership on a Blenheim raid on Bremen on 4 July 1941, Edwards' arrival coincided with that of Flt Lt Charles Patterson, who had also flown a tour on Blenheims (with No 114 Sqn):

'I was initially sent to a Boston unit, but I managed to get a transfer to Hughie Edwards' squadron. The Mosquito was an exciting new aeroplane, and it was everyones' ultimate aim and ambition to fly it. The rumour got about that it was able to fly unarmed across Europe and get away with it because it was as fast, if not faster, than the enemy fighters. It was such a wonderful aeroplane that it became everyones' dream in our little world to get on to a Mosquito unit. It was certainly mine.

'Edwards was legendary in No 2 Group not only for what he had done, but for what a wonderful individual he was. He made a tremendous impact just by his mere presence. The quality of his leadership was elusive, indescribable. It had something to do with his presence and ability to inspire. He was very imaginative and sensitive, but he placed a premium on efficiency and made it clear that this had two purposes. One was that the target must be hit, secondly, that crews should cover every possibility that would ensure their survival. He studied the tactics of survival combined with success to a greater degree than any other wing commander with whom I came into contact. He inspired crews not by appeals to their sense of duty and purpose, but through the supreme achievement of allowing them to conquer their fear. Far from playing down fear, he brought it into the open and made conquering it the ultimate goal. I didn't find this particular approach in any other leader I came across. He made no attempt to conceal his own fear.

'I think the best example I can give of this was when six crews, led by Edwards, were to go on a high level dawn raid on cities in the Ruhr at a time when casualties on this kind of operation were particularly heavy. We were sitting having breakfast in a naturally very gloomy atmosphere at about five in the morning when Tony Wickham, a young pilot officer going on his first trip, suddenly burst out and said, "I suppose this is a death or glory effort?" Well, pilot officers on their first trip were not supposed to speak on those occasions at all. Most of us reacted with slight disapproval, but Edwards lent forward, looked at him, and said, "There is no glory in it, and that's what makes it so worthwhile." The effect on all of us was electric, and we all went out feeling that we were going on a mission of supreme importance not to the war effort, but to ourselves and to our unit, and to show him that we could do it without thought of glory or reward, for its own sake.

'Mosquito operations were far more ambitious than Blenheim ops, but casualties were lower. When I first joined No 105 Sqn, the operations had not been properly worked out, and no one was sure of what the role for the Mosquito ought to be. It was being used at first for high level work, going out in broad daylight, unescorted, and bombing with a few bombs, and as a nuisance raider after a night raid – the latter idea was that the sirens would go and keep the workers' heads down and out of the factories. Well, it so happened that Bomber Command strategists had not made allowance for the Fw 190, which, at altitude, was slightly faster and certainly more manoeuvrable than the Mosquito Mk IV, which had the speed of the Spitfire. The Fw 190 was marginally faster than a Spitfire at this point in the war, and from July to September 1942, Mosquito casualties were as high as those suffered by Blenheim units performing low level daylight raids a year earlier. There was even talk of the Mosquito having to be written off after all. We still had such enormous faith in this aeroplane, however, and we refused to believe that it could not be made to operate successully with an acceptable rate of casualties.

'Hughie Edwards had hand-picked his flight commanders and his two deputy flight commanders – my flight commander was Peter Channer. The station commander, Gp Capt (later Air Chief Marshal Sir Wallace) Kyle, and "Eddie", had decided that to get the new crews blooded, they would organise a quick operation. So, on 5 August the target selected was the steelworks at Ijmuiden which, in the Blenheim era, had been regarded as a fierce target. Their idea of a training operation was to send off three new crews, or two new crews under a leader, in the morning, followed by two more in the afternoon against the same target with another leader.

'I was part of the afternoon sortie behind Flt Lt Roy Ralston, a fellow OTU instructor who had already reached a level of reverence throughout the whole of No 2 Group for his tremendous operational record on

Blenheims. Ralston was regarded by many, including Hughie Edwards, as the greatest bomber pilot of all time.

'A few days later I was told to report to the ops room. My route was up on the map. Even by Mosquito standards I was pretty appalled by what I saw. "Bomber" Harris wanted to know what the weather was like over Germany for a bombing raid that night because the "met" people were rather vague about it. It was a glorious, clear, September day, without a cloud in the sky over England. I was told to fly at 25,000 ft across the Dutch coast and fly straight to Magdeburg. I was then to turn for home, flying north-east past Berlin, up to Rostock and over north-west Denmark to Esbjerg, before returning back to England.

'Apart from anything else, this sortie would push the Mosquito to the limit of its range. I was told that I was the only Allied aircraft operating over Germany, so my chances of getting back seemed slim. To show how bad it was, "Eddie" said he was sorry that he had to send me on the mission, but that it had to be done. With a twinkle in his eye, he said, "You're not married you see, which is a factor we have to take into account".

'The challenge was so great that I didn't really have too much time to worry. As I climbed up to our operational ceiling I felt very "woozy", and I was having to really concentrate on the instruments – somehow my oxygen tube had been disconnected, and my navigator, Sgt Egan, had only noticed it when I was already up at nearly 25,000 ft. Quite suddenly, everything became clear. There in full view was the Dutch coast, with Holland spread out like a map in front of me. I felt absolutely normal. Such was "Eddie's" influence that it was purely the thought of him that made me keep going even when I was running out of oxygen at 25,000 ft.

'About half way to Magdeburg Egan quite suddenly screamed, "Snappers!" (enemy fighters). I threw the Mosquito into a vertical turning dive, thinking, "Oh my God, we've had it now". Then Egan told me, "Oh, I'm very sorry, it's only a fly!" I was so relieved and I resumed the flight. At our height you had to watch your back all the time so as to ensure that you where not letting out vapour trails. If you were, you had to drop height immediately. We carried on to Magdeburg in glorious blue sky – you could see for a hundred miles. When we turned north-east, mercifully we ran into cloud, which carried on till we were just short of Rostock, which was the most dangerous part of the trip. After we came out of this cloud there was blue sky and the Baltic spread out beneath us. We got to Esbjerg, and with a sigh of relief I dived down to sea level, and safety. It was nearly dusk when we got back to Horsham St Faith. A slightly flustered Hughie Edwards met us. He had heard nothing and had written us off.'

Soon after this mission Horsham St Faith was allocated to the USAAF as a Liberator base, so on 29 September Nos 105 and 139 Sqns began moving to their new station at Marham. The latter airfield had just been transferred from No 3 to No 2 Group, and would play a leading role in Mosquito operations until March 1944. F/L Charles Patterson recalls:

'Shortly after we moved to Marham the great glamour period of No 105 Sqn began. Edwards changed the tactics from high level daylight to low level daylight, bombing about 20 minutes before dark when it was light enough to identify the target, and then coming back under cover of growing darkness. This became the standard operation with the Mosquitoes, and it was highly successful.'

Flt Lt Victor Robson DFC* and Sqn Ldr D A G Parry DSO, DFC* pose in front of G for George of No 105 Sqn at Marham

THE 'SHALLOW DIVERS'

On 2 October 1942 six Mosquitoes from No 105 Sqn attacked Liège using a new type of tactic that would drastically improve the aircraft's bombing accuracy against pin-point targets. Apart from the 'traditional' low-level attack, crews were introduced to the 'shallow diving' method, the latter attack seeing the crew zoom down from 2000 to 1500 ft just prior to arriving over the target – their bombs were then released once they were at the lower altitude. With the availability of more B Mk IVs in 1943, this tactic would, on occasion, be used by the 'shallow divers' in conjunction with the first wave, who went in at low-level proper with 11-second delayed-action bombs. When this occurred, up to 20 Mosquitoes could cross the target almost simulataneously, as Charles Patterson vividly recalls:

'During October/November 1942 I did a number of exciting operations deep into Germany, going out at high level and coming back at low level, which was a most exhilerating experience. My splendid navigator was taken sick and removed, and I had to take whatever navigator was going, which usually meant one whom no-one else wanted. Having a navigator who (when flying low level in poor light), for 80 per cent of the time, hadn't the faintest idea where he was, added somewhat to the excitement. It also placed a much greater strain on my initiative and judgement.

'In the middle of November we all started to practice low level formation bombing day after day, whenever the weather permitted, for what we understood would be one of the major raids. The whole group was going to be involved, which meant that Venturas, Bostons and Mosquitoes would all have to operate together and arrive over the target simultaneously. Their differing operational speeds posed a planning headache, but this was not the worry of ordinary pilots like myself.

'On the morning of 20 November, Wg Cdr Edwards introduced me to Flg Off Jimmy Hill who, it was explained, was from the RAF Film Unit. He had a cine camera which was to be fitted into my Mosquito (DK338 'O-Orange'), and I was to take him on a low level recon-

No 105 Sqn's Sqn Ldr Roy Ralston DSO, DFM and Flt Lt Syd Clayton DFC, DFM are seen on 9 December 1942 following a very successful bombing raid which saw them lead two other B Mk IVs in a 'skip bombing' raid on the mouth of a French railway tunnel. The attack was designed to cause damage to both the tunnel and the track on the other side, thus making it difficult for the Germans to effect repairs

naissance of the Schelde Estuary. We would take a film of the route down the estuary, which the raiders would subsequently use on the forthcoming "big operation". This cine film would serve as an important navigational aid in the briefing of crews – particularly the lead navigators. When the actual operation took place a cine camera would,be carried for the first time. The powers-that-be told me that I would have to navigate myself, but that Hill had done a navigator's course.

'All we had to do was fly down the Schelde Estuary just over the Dutch mainland near Woensdrecht fighter airfield and back again, but we could not go in at low level. We had to go in at about 300 ft in order to get the correct angle for the cine camera to give a perspective of the islands ahead. By luck, and by dead reckoning, we arrived at the right point of entry, and Hill went down into the nose with his film camera. It was all very peaceful. We whizzed down the Schelde Estuary and crossed the mainland, and when I could see the hangars of Woensdrecht airfield on the horizon I turned sharply about and came home again. Well, they developed this film with a great deal of excitement. Both Gaumont British News and my pet spaniel were waiting when I landed, and the latter ended up on the news as well! Sadly, it soon became quite plain when the film was put on the projector that it was useless to navigators because the islands ahead looked just like any other islands along the Dutch coast.'

On 1 May 1943 Charles Patterson's DK338 took off for a raid on Eindhoven but lost an engine soon after take off and crashed near Marham, killing Flg Off O W Thompson DFC, RNZAF and Flg Off W J Horne DFC. The aircraft had successfully completed 23 sorties.

Top and above
The No 2 Group attack on the Philips Stryp Group main works at Eindhoven, Holland, is seen in progress on 6 December 1942. Some 84 bombers, including 11 B Mk IVs (eight from No 105 Sqn and two from No 139), took part in Operation *Oyster*, as the mission was code-named. The Mosquito force, led by Wg Cdr Hughie Edwards VC, DFC made a shallow diving attack on the Stryp works, while the other bombers dropped their ordnance from low level. No 139 Sqn's Sqn Ldr J E Houlston AFC, DFC carried out bomb damage assessment in the immediate aftermath of the raid

OPERATION *OYSTER*

On 6 December 1942 Operation *Oyster* saw 84 Mosquito, Boston and Ventura bombers from No 2 Group attack the Philips Stryp Group main works and the Emmasingel valve and lamp factory in Eindhoven, Holland. Ten Mosquitoes (eight Mk IVs of No 105 Sqn and two from No 139 Sqn), led by Wg Cdr Hughie Edwards VC, DFC made a shallow diving attack on the Stryp works, while the other bombers dropped their ordnance from low level. Sqn Ldr J E Houlston AFC, DFC of No 139

No 105 Sqn line up at Marham on 11 December 1942. The closest aircraft, DZ360/A, failed to return from Termonde just 11 days later, with the loss of Flt Sgt J E Cloutier and Sgt A C Foxley; DZ353/E was lost on 9 June 1944 (see page 8); DZ367/J was downed during a raid to Berlin on 30 January 1943; DK336/P lost its starboard engine returning from a raid on Copenhagen on 27 January 1943, then struck a balloon cable and a tree and crashed at Yaxham, in Norfolk, killing Sgt R Clare and Flg Off E Doyle; DZ378/K was withdrawn from service after only two sorties following damage inflicted on 20 December 1942; and PZ379/H was lost on 17 August 1943 whilst flying with No 139 Sqn on a diversionary mission to Berlin for the famous Peenemünde raid – the Mosquito, which was downed by a nightfighter, carried both Flg Off A S Cook (an American pilot from Wichita Falls, Texas) and navigator, Sgt D A H Dixon, to their deaths

Sqn carried out bomb damage assessment. Charles Patterson again:

'Operationally, the Philips works raid from a Mosquito point of view was regarded as a comparatively straightforward target – nothing to get terribly frightened about, and something we would have taken in our stride as part of routine operations. I flew in the second formation of four Mosquitoes (in DZ414 'O for Orange') as No 3 to Sqn Ldr George Parry, who was a very famous Mosquito pilot, and one of our flight commanders. We followed Edwards' formation of six.

'Our attack was supposedly timed so that we didn't get involved with either the Venturas or Bostons. Our concern was that should we get tangled up with either type, we would have to reduce speed, which of course from a Mosquito point of view was dangerous because we had no defensive armament. We were to fly to somewhere just south of Eindhoven, turn to port, and then attack the target. The Mosquitoes were to climb to 1500 ft just short of the target and then shallow dive on to it because it was assumed that Bostons would have hit it at low level before us – Hill would film the target with his cine camera. This sounded an interesting thing to do because for once there would be a chance of seeing what we'd done afterwards.

'We flew across the Dutch coast at low level. The thing I remember most clearly was looking across my port wing tip and seeing Fw 190s literally in a line taking off from Woensdrecht to intercept us. They only looked about 200-300 yards away – it was actually about half a mile. They looked so normal, just like Spitfires taking off in England, that it was hard to believe they were coming up to kill you. We had to slow right down as we found ourselves getting involved with some Venturas. We ended up not far above our stalling speed as we tried to get behind them.'

Showing both coolness and decisiveness, Sqn Ldr George Parry and his No 2, Flt Lt Bill Blessing, broke away so as to draw the Fw 190s onto themselves, but they eventually lost them as they accelerated to full speed. Parry later rejoined the formation, but Blessing had to return to base.

'The Fw 190s couldn't resist it when they saw these two turn round, and they duly fell for Parry's deception, leaving us alone. The Mk IV was slower than the Fw 190 at 20,000 ft, but at deck level it was 5 mph faster.

'There were no more fighter interceptions. Ahead of me I saw the front formation of Mosquitoes in the distance already climbing up to 1500 ft, so I immediately took my formation up as fast as I could in order to catch

Edwards' formation. We caught up about two to three miles south of Eindhoven. He banked over to port and started to dive down on the Philips works in the centre of the town. The moment I turned to port I could see the factory prominantly standing out right in the centre of Eindhoven. We all went down in a shallow dive at full throttle, and at the appropriate moment dropped the bombs. As I went across the Philips works the factory seemed to erupt in a cloud of smoke and flashes. It looked as though the whole thing had been completely destroyed.

'In the distance I could see masses of Bostons whizzing about across the trees at low level to port. I came straight down to ground level. Now the Mosquitoes split up and we all had to come home separately. It was now noon on a lovely sunny day, with virtually no cloud, so I set off across the Dutch countryside at high speed. I decided not to follow the given route out, which was towards the coast of Holland and out into the North Sea. I decided that that was where the fighters would be, waiting for the main formation, so I therefore turned north towards the Zuider Zee. Plt Off J E O'Grady, who was on his first trip (with Sgt G W Lewis), latched on to me to see him home. He followed me all the way up the Zuider Zee, and I knew we'd made it when we whizzed over the Causeway at about 20 ft.

'I turned to port to come out between Den Helder and Texel. This was a mistake on my part because the light flak sites at Den Helder and on the southern tip of Texel were sufficiently close enough to hit you should you fly between them. I therefore had to cross a belt of light flak and weaving tracer as I flew between the two islands, but I emerged unscathed. I took the usual evasive action, and the Mosquito behind appeared to be perfectly all right. However, when we were about six minutes out into the North Sea, Hill said, "He's gone into the sea!" At first I could not believe what he was saying because we were now some 30 miles out to sea, but

B Mk IV Series II DZ367/J of No 139 Sqn is bombed up in preparation for a raid – note that the aircraft's shrouded exhausts have scorched the cowlings. One of three No 139 Sqn aircraft sent to bomb Berlin in an attempt to disrupt a speech being made by Nazi propaganda minister, Dr Joseph Goebbels, on the afternoon of 30 January 1943, this Mosquito lost and its crew were during the daring daylight raid

when I turned round and went back it was only too true. All that remained of the Mosquito was a big, boiling, cauldron of water. O'Grady was a nice, cheerful, young Canadian. I'd known him as a pupil at OTU at Upwood when I was an instructor. He only looked about 16 – I suppose he was about 20. I momentarily felt guilty, for if I'd done something different, and he hadn't followed me, he'd still be alive.

'When the film was developed half of it was spoiled in the laboratory, which made both Hughie Edwards and I absolutely livid (in total, more than 60 tons of bombs had hit the Philips factories, which were very badly damaged, but 14 aircraft had been lost). Unbeknown to me, Eindhoven turned out to be the beginning of a new operational role that I was to perform for a long time. A month later I was sent to Hatfield to test fly three Mosquitoes and pick out one that I thought had the best performance. Whilst I was there Sir Geoffrey de Havilland treated me as an honoured guest. I chose DZ414, which was allotted to the RAF Film Unit (FU). Coded 'O-Orange', I was to fly it for 20,000 of its 24,000 miles.'

Charles Patterson then returned to Marham, and No 105 Squadron:

'Christmas came and went and the weather turned bad in January 1943, so I only did two ops. We all settled down to practice for a low level daylight attack on the Burmeister and Wain submarine building yards at Copenhagen, but at this time there was a sudden sweep of rumours. A change in the Mosquito force was planned, and any crew could volunteer to join a new formation in Bomber Command called the Pathfinders. It would mean promotion and an interesting new job. I had now been four months on my second tour so I thought I would try a change.

'I duly joined No 109 Sqn at Wyton, but I discovered that the Mosquito was going to fly on instruments at 30,000 ft at night and mark targets using *Oboe*. The attitude of everyone there was simply antipathetic to my outlook because they regarded themselves as the elite, whereas none of them had actually flown operations that were anything like as dangerous, daring or comprehensive as we'd been doing in No 2 Group – I didn't much care for the chaps there, and I certainly didn't like the job. I undertook one night film operation using DZ414 during my time as a Pathfinder, but this was a futile effort because to the public, every target at night looked the same. So it was decided to return the FU Mosquito back to No 105 Sqn and make low level daylight films with it instead.'

The raid on the Burmeister and Wain works went ahead on 27 January 1943, with Wg Cdr Edwards leading nine B Mk IVs of Nos 105 and 139

No 139 Sqn armourers check that the recently loaded bombs have been correctly fitted into the belly of Mosquito DZ464 at Marham in the early spring of 1943. This aircraft was lost just days later on 21 May 1943 when it was downed by flak over the French coast following a bombing raid on the locomotive sheds at Orleans. Former acting squadron OC, Sqn Ldr V R G Harcourt DFC, RCAF, and his navigator, Wt Off O J Friendly DFM RCAF, were killed in the crash

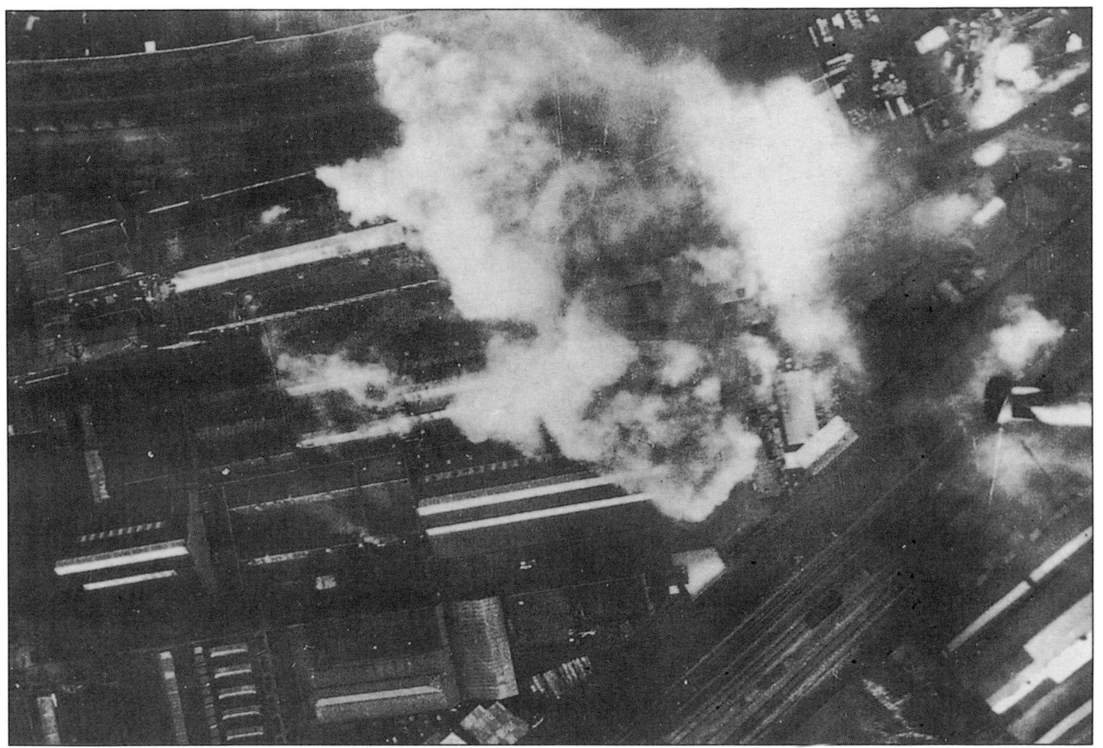

Mid February 1943 became known as the 'Great Tours Derby' for the aircrew of Nos 105 and 139 Sqns. On the afternoon of 14 February the engine sheds in the French city were attacked from low level by six of the ten Mosquitoes despatched by No 139 Sqn. The following evening, 12 Mosquitoes from No 105 Sqn bombed the Tours goods depot in a low-level raid, and on the 18th a dozen B Mk IVs made a shallow diving attack on the same target (pictured here) – two aircraft aborted and one Mosquito failed to return

Sqns. Light flak from ships positioned along the coast bracketed the formation on the way in, leaving Flt Lt J Gordon DFC and Flg Off R G Hayes DFC thinking that their aircraft had been hit when the trailing edge of their starboard wing became enveloped in blue smoke. However, Gordon had actually clipped a telegraph line whilst carrying out evasive action in an effort to put the German gunners off their aim. He quickly turned around and headed home with a damaged port aileron – both men were subsequently killed in a crash whilst attempting to return on one engine from an operation to Leverkusen on 5 November 1943.

Edwards and Cairns found their target just as they too were on the point of returning, but they swiftly dropped their bombs and broke for the sea – and home. Light flak around the yards was intense, claiming the Mosquito flown by Sgts J G Dawson and R H Cox – Edwards' aircraft returned with two holes in the starboard nacelle.

On 30 January Mosquitoes bombed Berlin in two attacks, the first (in the morning) involving three Mk IVs of No 105 Sqn, led by Sqn Ldr 'Reggie' W Reynolds and Plt Off E B 'Ted' Sismore, and the second (in the afternoon) a trio of aircraft from No 139 Sqn. Both raids were timed to disrupt speeches being given at the main broadcasting station by Reichsmarschall Herman Göring and Dr Joseph Goebbels. No 105 Sqn arrived over Berlin at exactly 1100 hours, their bombs disrupting Göring's speech for over an hour. Sadly, the second raid was not as successful, with Sqn Ldr D F W Darling DFC being shot down and killed.

Whilst all this was going on Charles Patterson eased his way back into operations with No 105 Sqn again after his brief sojourn in No 8 Group;

'They had been going "great-guns" during February-March, demonstrating how the Mosquito could go in at zero feet on a regular basis and

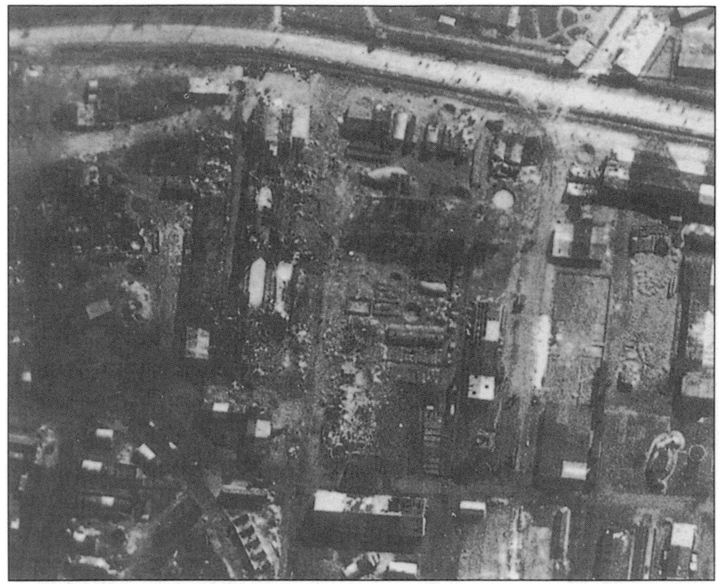

Precision bombing at its best – the U-boat Supply Depot at Rennes after the low level attack by 16 Mosquitoes of Nos 105 and 139 Sqns on 26 February 1943. Leading the raid was No 105 Sqn's newly-appointed OC, Wg Cdr G P Longfield (with navigator Flt Lr R F Millns), in DZ365/V. Both men were killed when their aircraft collided with DZ413/K, crewed by Flg Offs S G Kimmel and H N Kirkland, RCAF, whilst attempting to avoid flak over the target area

get back with at least an acceptable rate of casualties. Then No 139 Sqn began specialising in a new form of attack, climbing to 1500 ft and doing a shallow dive down on to the target in the wake of the low level Mosquitoes from No 105 Sqn. The latter unit now had a new squadron commander called John Wooldridge – a rather flamboyant character who had done an enormous number of trips in heavy bombers. He had a DFC and two Bars, and a large moustache!'

Hughie Edwards had left No 105 Sqn in February to take up a post at HQ Bomber Command, but his successor, Wg Cdr G P Longfield, only lasted a matter of days as he was killed in a mid-air collision on 26 February 1943. Wg Cdr John de Lacy Wooldridge DFC, DFM assumed command of the unit on 17 March and went on to lead No 105 Sqn on many low level raids – for which he was duly awarded a DSO and a bar to his DFC. Charles Patterson again:

'During the next two or three months I went off on a few "low levels", one of which was a very long one indeed (on a fine afternoon on 2 May) to the railway repair workshops at Thionville, near Metz. We flew at low level in eight Mosquitoes led by Reggie Reynolds, who was a new flight commander with Wellington experience, and Ted Sismore, who'd developed into an absolutely brilliant navigator. We flew ar low level across the Channel. Of course, flying the FU Mosquito I was always near the back – three from the end, flying No 5, with two aircraft in starboard echelon. We were always in a starboard echelon because the aircraft's response to the throttles opening and shutting was so lethargic. This meant that the Mosquito could not decelerate safely, only accelerate, so we always flew in echelon rather than a vic. This problem also negated any chance the pilot had of manoeuvering at low level when on the outside of a turn.

'As we came up over the cliffs we encountered some light flak. It seemed to be getting very near to me, so when I judged that the moment was right, I pulled on the stick and went up about 100 ft. As I did so, the flak shot under me and hit the starboard engine of the chap to my left, causing the aircraft to emit a large black cloud of smoke. The crew then feathered the engine and went back home on one. I resumed my normal position.

'We flew right across northern France, north-west of Paris, and down to Soissons – mile after mile at low level, across the green fields of France. Then we banked due east to come up to Thionville, which lay some 20 miles south, before turning to port in an effort to avoid any chance of us missing the target by flying too far north or south. These were always the tactics used, and of course we did "dog legs", never flying in one direction for more than 20 minutes. As a result, we reached Thionville without a shot being fired. We raced up on the target, with Reynolds in the leading aircraft opening up the throttles. He wouldn't go across the target flat out (the leader wouldn't do that), but he'd go up to about 300, and then he'd give the order to open the bomb doors. Then the target came up and everyone went for it. You were over it and gone in a flash. We achieved complete surprise, which allowed us to get across the target and deliver our bombs right on the mark. The last pilot over said he thought he saw a gun open fire.

'Now the really interesting part of the trip arrived. Instead of turning back north-west to fly across France and Belgium, we carried out the highly imaginative idea of heading due north, knowing that the Germans would assume that we must be coming back across north-west France – they would be sending their fighters down to that area to meet us before it got dark, so to fox them we flew north. It was an extraordinary sensation flying across the mountains of Luxembourg and the forests of the Ardennes at low level, before crossing into Germany. It seemed endless, and then in the gathering gloom we suddenly shot across the banks of the Rhine and up across Holland – I came out between Ameland and Vlieland. Flying over the Causeway at the top of the Zuider Zee, I knew I was on course for home.'

An enemy flak gun emplacement opens up on a Mosquito during a low level attack by four B Mk IVs of No 105 Sqn on the Stork Diesel Works at Hengelo, in Holland, on 28 February 1943. The flying debris in the foreground is from a bomb that had just burst through the roof of the Manemeyer electrical and mechanical equipment factory. The train passing behind the flak gun emplacement is travelling along the Derventer to Zwolle railway line

BOMBS ON THE 'BIG CITY'

Just prior to the Thionville raid, No 105 Sqn was involved in a hastily arranged surprise bombing attack on Berlin on the night of 20/21 April 1943. One of the pilots involved was Charles Patterson:

'The primary reason for this mission was to "celebrate" Hitler's birthday by delivering a suitable "present" to him. As this date coincided with a full moon, Bomber Command planners had enough sense to know that the Mosquito possessed the range to get to Berlin and back in moonlight conditions. Eight of us went on this attack. It was the most brilliant moonlight night, and the flight was a very long one – over four hours, of which roughly three would be spent over enemy territory. We had to constantly keep a lookout for fighters because the moon was so bright, weaving and turning so that our navigators could look back for them. The moon would catch and reflect on the wings and on the perspex, and looking down, all the lakes were lit up with the reflection of the moon. I don't think that this trip worried anybody, It certainly didn't worry me. To go over Germany at high level at night in a Mosquito seemed almost as safe as flying over England, provided you kept out of the way of any fighters.

'Berlin was not difficult to pick out thanks to the vast "blackness" of the city and the Potsdam lakes. I was at about 18,000 ft and settled down to do a straight and level run. The only thing about this attack was that we felt it was slightly "second class" when compared with the daylight raid that we had done a few months before. We resented being sent on such a mission as it was not taken very seriously by Bomber Command.

'Suddenly, there were flashes and black puffs of flak. I remember thinking "this is not what you get in a Mosquito – you're too fast for this sort of thing" – and then just before I dropped my bombs there was a violent bump. I thought it outrageous that one could be downed at night in a Mosquito. It was just not done. It was unsporting and not good form at all.

'Anyway, we turned round and weaved our way back across northern Germany and over the Dutch coast in the direction of home – we were bathed in brilliant moonlight throughout the operation. We had one loss – Wg Cdr Peter Shand, OC No 139 Sqn (and his navigator, Plt Off C D Handley DFM), who we subsequently heard had been downed (by Oberleutnant Lothar Linke of IV./NJG 1) on the way home.

Wg Cdr John de Lacy Wooldridge DFC*, DFM, took over command of No 105 Sqn on 17 March 1943. He is seen here posing in the emergency roof exit hatch of his personal Mosquito B Mk IV, *KNAVE OF DIAMONDS*. Note the two-piece front windscreen, which was soon replaced by a bullet-proof fighter style flat windscreen, and the direct vision panel (forward of the blister), which opened inwards on each side. Wooldridge joined the RAF in 1938 and flew two tours on heavy bombers (including 32 ops on the ill-fated Manchester with Nos 61, 207 and 106 Sqns) prior to taking command of No 105 Sqn. He survived the war only to die in a car accident in 1958

'Once back on the ground, we were debriefed and went to bed. When I went up to the flights the next morning I was asked if I had realised that I had been hit the night before? I said, "No. I had a bump and realised that there had been a burst fairly close. I didn't know I had been hit. I suppose there are just a few tiny little holes in the wing or something?" They said, "Oh no, You've virtually had it". A piece of shrapnel had gone right through the tail of the Mosquito where the elevator wires all link up with the tailplane and the rudder. All but one of these wires had been totally severed, the sole intact strand on a single control line allowing me fly the Mosquito as if nothing had happened. I was unaware that anything was wrong at all as the aircraft had handled perfectly.

'Although we were ignorant of it at the time, this night attack was to set the pattern for Mosquito operations for the rest of the war. Harris and his Bomber Command staff were very taken with the idea that they could send a force of bombers to Berlin any night of the year, regardless of the moon, and it resulted in Nos 105 and 139 Sqns being retained in Bomber Command when No 2 Group went into the 2nd Tactical Air Force – this was a severe setback for both units.

THE JENA RAID

On 27 May 1943 an operation was laid on for Nos 105 and 139 Sqns which would mark the end of the great low level daylight raids for RAF Bomber Command. Participating crews were unaware of the mission's significance at the time, as Charles Patterson recalls:

'We were all called into the crewroom at about 2 o'clock one afternoon and told that there was to be a major operation. We saw the red route marker ribbon running longer than we'd ever considered right down into south-east Germany, near Leipzig. The target was soon revealed as the Zeiss optical lens works at Jena which, at that time, was engaged almost exclusively in making periscopes for submarines.'

The operation called for eight B Mk IVs of No 105 Sqn to hit the Zeiss factory while six No 139 Sqn Mosquitoes bombed the nearby Schott Glass Works. Patterson again:

'It gave me a great sense of anticipation and excitement that such a tremendously long trip was going to be undertaken, but equally did not cause me undue alarm because it was so deep into Germany – an area that had never seen daylight flying aircraft before. We rather assumed that by going "deep down" not only could we achieve a great deal of surprise, but there might not be much AA fire around the factory – we also believed that any flak sites in the area would be manned by inexperienced gunners.

'The BBC came to do an outside broadcast of the whole thing. The briefing was both long and complicated. It meant flying at low level over enemy territory for well over three hours – a good two-and-a-quarter hours of which would be in broad daylight. I was the Film Unit pilot, and Flt Sgt Leigh Howard was my camerman-navigator. When the briefing was over we went back to the hangars, after which followed an extraordinarily long period of waiting for the right time to go down to the aircraft and strap in. It was a gloriously clear and hot, but slightly misty, late May evening. The timing of the take-offs to get the whole formation into the air had to be precise, so there had been a synchronisation of watches. We all settled into our aircraft ten minutes prior to start up so as to ensure that everyone was aboard.

'The time had arrived. Wg Cdr Reynolds was going to lead with Sismore. We saw the flash of his exhaust and his engines started. At 7 o'clock engines fired up around the perimeter and everybody taxied out. Forming up on these trips was a lengthy business, the leader circling slowly round the airfield waiting for everybody to get airborne and catch up. Here I was again with this damn camera, going on another major trip at the end of my second tour, and flying near the back of not the first, but the second, formation.

'The two formations swept across the hangars and the airfield at low level, which made for an impressive sight, and quite an exhilerating ex-

This daring roof top attack on the St Joseph Locomotive Works in Nantes on 23 March 1943 was timed to perfection so as to allow factory workers to have vacated the site prior to the first bombs being dropped. The raid was carried out by three B Mk IVs of No 105 Sqn, led by Wg Cdr Peter Shand DFC, and eight aircraft from No 139 Sqn, led by Sqn Ldr Bill Blessing DSO, DFC, RAAF (who was later killed in action on 7 July 1944 on a 'Path Finder Force' marking sortie over Caen). Shand led two more outstandingly successful attacks against the molybdenum mines at Knaben, in Norway, on 3 March, and on Eindhoven some 27 days later. He and his navigator, Plt Off C D Handley DFM, were lost on the night bombing attack on Berlin on 20/21 April 1943 when their Mosquito was shot down by Oberleutnant Lothar Linke of IV./NJG 1 over Ijsselmeer during their return trip home

Wg Cdr R W Reynolds DSO, DFC (at right) assumes command of No 139 Sqn (note the unit's 'Jamaica Squadron' crest above the doorway at RAF Marham) in May 1943 from acting OC, Sqn Ldr V R G Harcourt, RCAF

perience for the crews themselves. We settled down for the long flight across to Jena in clear daylight, as it was certainly a good two hours before dusk. The Dutch coast was crossed with no difficulty, but at the Zuider Zee we suddenly found ourselves flying slap into a vast fleet of little brown-sailed fishing vessels. In front of me the whole formation broke up and weaved in and around them, before we settled down again. On past the Ruhr and down near Kassel we went, then on into the Thuringian mountains, where the Möhne and Eder dams are. Even then we were only two-thirds of the way. You felt you were in a different world which has no end and will go on forever. On and on over the trees, fields and rising ground we went, mile after mile. Then, suddenly, my navigator drew my attention to something. I looked across the starboard wingtip and could clearly see Münster cathedral some miles away – the interesting thing was that I was looking *up* at the towers, not down on them!

'We carried on past Kassel, then, suddenly, we came across all the floods of the Möhne dam raid which had taken place just ten days before. For 20 minutes there was nothing but floods. It was fascinating to see, and confirmed in our minds what an enormous success the raid must have been. We flew between the Möhne and Eder dams and suddenly came over a mountain ridge and there was a dam beneath us. On the far side the front formation was just topping the far ridge when flak opened up – it didn't look very serious. However, an enormous ball of flame rolled down the mountainside, which was obviously an aircraft, and it wasn't long before that I learnt that *two* Mosquitoes had collided (crewed by Flt Lt Sutton/Flg Off Morris and Flg Off Openshaw/Sgt Stonestreet, both from No 139 Sqn). Whether one was hit by flak, or the presence of enemy fire had caused one of the pilots to take his eyes off what he was doing and fly into the Mosquito next to him, nobody will ever know, but two had gone.

'We flew on over the mountainous country, along ridges and down long valleys with houses on both sides. We saw a man open his front door on my starboard wingtip and look out to see us flashing past his house. We then saw the door slam in a flash as we whipped past.

Suddenly, the weather began to deteriorate, which had not been forecast. I think everybody was assuming that we'd soon fly out of it, but it got worse and and we were still over mountains. We now began to fly right into clouds. Blessing put on his navigation lights to try and enable us to keep formation, and everybody followed suit, and although I did my best to keep the next aircraft in view, I lost him. I found myself flying alone, so I wondered what was going to happen to everybody else. When I came out of the cloud the visibility was poor. It was grey and gloomy, and Howard had no idea where he was. The only thing to do was to turn for home and see if I could pick up something which was worth bombing.

'So I set off, lost in the sense that I'd no idea where we actually were. The only thing to do was to stick to the flight plan and steer north-east to come up north of Hanover, by which time it should be getting dark, and then fly west across the Hanoverian plain into the night. I'd only been flying a very short time when suddenly I approached what was clearly a very large town. In view of the low cloud base at about 800-1000 ft, and the limited visibility, I felt quite safe. If any fighters appeared, I could pop into the cloud. There was no sign of a factory – it was a residential town, so I assumed there wasn't much flak about. I flew right round and noticed a large railway station in the centre, which our maps told us was Weimar.

'I pointed the nose slightly down, opened up to full throttle and went into a medium steep dive straight at the station. I opened the bomb doors and dropped my ordnance straight into the station from about 200 ft. I couldn't miss.

'More tracer came up from the sides of the hills. I pulled the stick back and yawed to port, then pushed it down and yawed to starboard, trying never to keep a constant pattern of behaviour. Then at last we emerged from this ordeal. I felt rather shaken by it. I didn't even bother to consult my navigator because I knew he'd be palpitating like a jelly. He was a pre-war Pinewoods or Denham studio cameraman who'd suddenly found himself in this horrifying position. There I was in the middle of Germany, unsure of my position, and having no clear idea of what course to steer to get home, which was a hell of a long way away. It was quite a daunting prospect, but there was no point in panicking. This was the sole occasion during my wartime flying that I felt both isolated and apprehensive.

'The return was in fact quite traumatic. After landing, I discovered that the target had been attacked, and that one or two Mosquitoes were coming back badly shot up – the flak over the target was worse than I'd thought. Both formations had hit the target without me, so I thought that I'd put up a rather a bad show. They had attacked in deplorable visibility, flying through a balloon barrage over the factory itself. Wg Cdr Reynolds got back, but his aircraft was badly shot up and he had been wounded. His navigator had bound up his injuries, and they'd had to fly back on one engine, plus had got lost. They had flown over some heavily defended areas and been hit again, and Reynolds only just got the aircraft back. He came into the crewroom looking rather washed out and with his arm nestled in a sling.

'The factory had been hit, but just how much damage had been done we didn't know. We had lost five out of fourteen aircraft, so the reaction to the raid was mixed. It was regarded as a tremendous tactical achievement, but the casualties had been worse than expected. After the Jena raid, No 2 Group was kept in Bomber Command (Nos 105 and 139 Sqns were now transferred to No 8 Pathfinder Group for a complete change of role), whilst the rest joined Grp Capt Basil Embry as part of the Tactical Air Force. The Mosquitoes were put onto night bombing, a role which had caught Harris' imagination during our first Berlin trip.'

THE PATHFINDERS

In No 8 Group (PFF), No 105 Sqn would operate alongside No 109 Sqn as the second *Oboe* (a high-level blind bombing radar aid) marker unit, while No 139 Sqn became the 'supporting squadron', going in with the markers themselves. These three units formed the backbone of Air Commodore (later AVM) Donald C T Bennett's specialist Pathfinder Force, which had been formed in August 1942, and increased in size until it achieved group status on 13 January 1943. The PFF markers' job was to 'illuminate' and 'mark' targets with coloured TI's (target indicators) for both the Main Force of 'heavies' and other No 8 Group Mosquitoes. No 109 Sqn had joined No 8 Group at Wyton on 1 June 1942, and *Oboe* had first been used on 20/21 December 1942 when then OC, Sqn Ldr H E 'Hal' Bufton, and his navigator, Flt Lt E L Ifould (along with two other crews), bombed a power-station in Holland.

On 31 December 1942/1 January 1943, sky-marking using *Oboe* was tried for the first time when two Mosquitoes of No 109 Sqn provided the TIs for eight Lancasters of the Pathfinder Force sent to bomb Düsseldorf. Sky markers were parachute flares deployed to pick a spot in the sky in the

An ex-Imperial Airways and Atlantic ferry pilot, Australian AVM Donald C T Bennett (centre), C-in-C No 8 Group (PFF), is seen here with his staff officers at a briefing session. Formed originally from No 3 Group using volunteer crews, No 8 Group started life as a specialist PFF force on 15 August 1942, before achieving fully-fledged group status on 13 January 1943. By March 1945 No 8 Group controlled some 19 squadrons, 10 of which were equipped with Mosquitoes

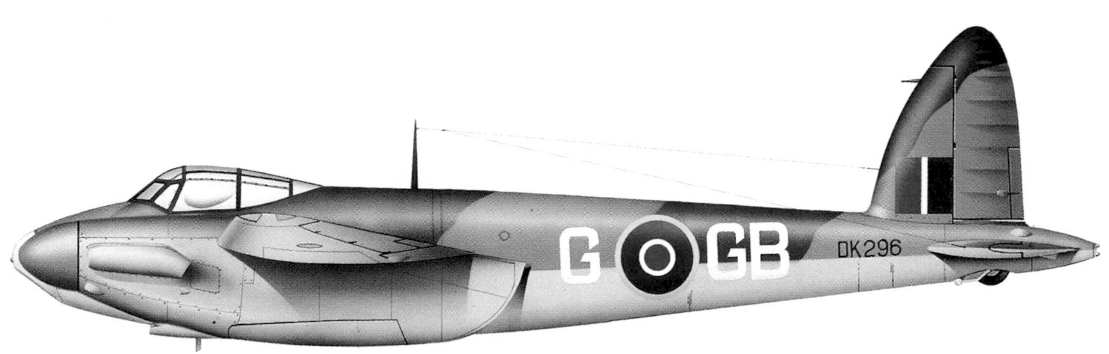

1
B Mk IV Series II DK296/GB-G of No 105 Sqn, No 2 Group, flown by Flt Lt D A G 'George' Parry DFC and Flg Off V Robson, 1/2 June 1942

Highly-polished for extra speed, DK296 made its operational debut on 1/2 June 1942 in the wake of the 'Thousand Bomber' raid on Cologne. On 11 July 'G-George' was badly damaged when Sgt P W R Rowland flew so low on the raid on Flensburg that he hit a roof and returned with pieces of chimney pot lodged in the aircraft's nose. On 25 September Parry and Robson used DK296 to lead an attack by four Mosquitoes on the Gestapo HQ in Oslo. 'G-George' was then passed on to Sqn Ldr Bill Blessing DSO, DFC, RAAF, who crash-landed it at Marham and broke its back. The aircraft was duly repaired, and was issued to No 305 Ferry Training Unit at Errol, in Scotland, where it was used to train Soviet crews who were converting onto Albermarles. On 20 April 1944 DK296 was ferried to the Soviet Union by a Russian crew, subsequently serving with the Red Air Force. Its ultimate fate is unknown.

2
B Mk IV Series II DZ414/O of the FPU, flown by Flt Lt C E S Patterson, 14 February 1943

Flt Lt C E S Patterson selected DZ414 for service with the FPU. He subsequently flew it for 20,000 of its 24,000 miles, including its debut operation to Lorient on 14 February 1943 in the wake of the 466-bomber raid staged the night before, the night bombing attack on Berlin on 20/21 April 1943 (performed to coincide with Hitler's birthday), when DZ414 was badly damaged by flak, the raids on Turin and Nürnburg, and on the long-range operation to Jena on 27 May. The second 'B' on the nose is for the Berlin operation on 13/14 May 1943. Whilst part of the 2nd TAF, DZ414 took part in many notable operations, including 14 anti-Diver sorties flown by Flt Lt Vic Hester of No 613 Sqn, along with cameraman, Flg Off Oakley, between 19-25 June 1944. It also participated in the Amiens prison raid on 18 February 1944, its pilot Flt Lt Tony Wickham, making three passes over the burning prison so as to allow Plt Off Leigh Howard to film the flight of 255 of the 700 prisoners released through the breached walls. Finally, on 21 March 1945 DZ414 was flown by Flt Lt K L Greenwood of No 487 Sqn, RNZAF, as part of the force sent on the Shellhaus raid, Flg Off E Moore of the FPU filming the first wave attack on the building. Despite is wartime contribution, this veteran machine was struck off charge in October 1946 and unceremoniously scrapped.

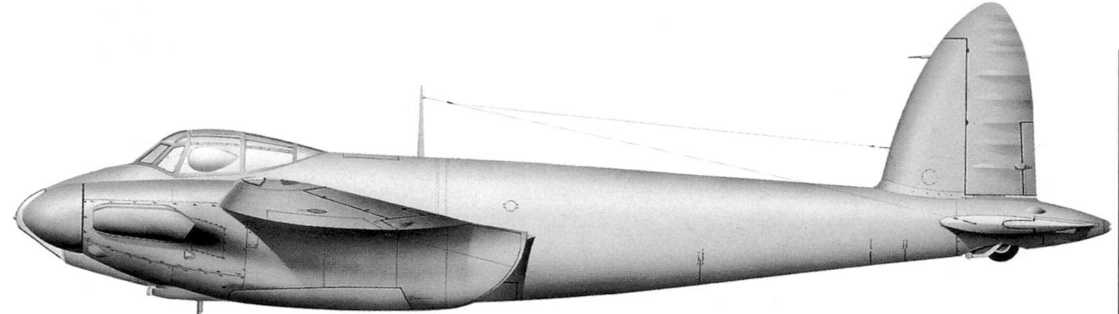

3
B Mk IV Series II DK301, No 105 Sqn, flown by Flt Lt D A G Parry and Flg Off V Robson, August 1942

Stripped of its camouflage scheme, codes, serial, and national insignia, and painted overall pale grey, this aircraft was used by Parry and Robson for the first Mosquito diplomatic run to Stockholm, via Leuchars, on 4 August 1942, the crew deliver-ing mail and cyphers for the British Embassy. Whilst airborne on a training flight on 8 November 1942, pilot Flt Sgt N Booth was unable to lower the undercarriage and DK301 belly-landed in a field at Abbey Farm, near RAF Marham. The aircraft was struck off charge nine days later.

4
B Mk IV DZ476/XD-S of No 139 Sqn, flown by Flt Lt G S W Rennie, RCAF, and Flg Off W Embry, RCAF, 4 March 1943

This Canadian pair flew as one of the 'shallow diver' crews on raids to the railway engine sheds at Aulnoye on 4 March 1943 (a flak burst during this trip hit the fuselage and severed the rudder control cables), to the John Cockerill Steel and Armament Works at Liège on 12 March, and to the engine sheds at Paderborn four days later. DZ476 remained with No 139 Sqn until it was lost in a crash at Upwood on 1 January 1944.

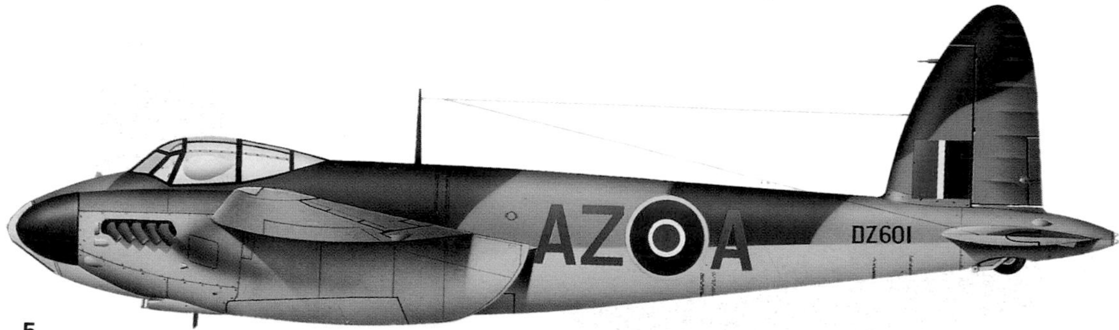

5
B Mk IV Series II DZ601/AZ-A, No 627 Sqn, No 5 Group, flown by Flg Off J F Thomson DFC, RNZAF, and Flg Off B E B Harris, Woodhall Spa, May 1944

Prior to its arrival at No 627 Sqn, this aircraft had been used for the raid on the Schott Glass Works at Jena on 27 May 1943 – it had suffered flak damage to its port engine propeller blade during the operation.On 24 May 1944 it was issued to No 627 Sqn at Woodhall Spa, where it became AZ-A. On 28 May 1944, whilst crewed by Flg Offs J F Thomson DFC, RNZAF, and B E B Harris, DZ601 was one of four Mosquitoes to drop target indicators on the gun batteries at St Martin de Varreville for Lancasters of No 5 Group. Three days later, after returning from a raid on the Saumur marshalling yards, Thomson and Harris had to belly-land DZ601 after its port engine over-revved and would not feather. Although the aircraft was repaired, it flew no more operational sorties.

6
B Mk IV DZ421 Series II/XD-G of No 139 Sqn, flown by the OC, Wg Cdr Peter Shand and Plt Off C D Handley DFM, Marham, early 1943

Shand and Handley flew this aircraft regularly until they were shot down and killed over Berlin in DZ386 by Oberleutnant Lothar Linke of IV./NJG 1 on the night of 20/21 April 1943. DZ421 was transferred to No 627 Sqn on 21 April 1944, where it was re-coded AZ-C. Like DZ601, this aircraft also participated in the St Martin de Varreville operation, its crew on this occasion being Flt Lts R L Bartley DFC and J O Mitchell, RCAF. Sent for repairs soon after this raid, DZ421 then went to No 1655 Mosquito Training Unit, where it was lost on 25 July 1944 when it broke up in flight.

7
B Mk IX *Oboe* LR507/GB-F of No 109 Sqn, No 8 Group (PFF), Wyton, 17 June 1943

This aircraft served with No 109 Sqn for just 18 days between 17 June and 5 July 1943, when it was reassigned to No 105 Sqn. Paired up with LR506 for its first mission (flown on 13/14 July), LR507 carried out a diversionary operation dropping target indicators (TIs) over Cologne for the Main Force attack on Aachen. On 10/11 April 1944, LR507 (and RV322) dropped TIs for the first of three waves of Mosquitoes involved in a 77-aircraft strong raid on Berlin.

8
B Mk XVI ML942/P3-D of No 692 Sqn, No 8 Group (PFF), Graveley, March 1944

This aircraft spent its entire career in No 8 Group (PFF), moving to No 692 Sqn at Graveley on 13 March 1944. Early in April, ML942 joined No 571 Sqn working up at Graveley, and was one of two aircraft to undertake the first squadron operation on 12/13 April 1944. Sent to bomb Osnabruck with a single 4000-lb 'Cookie', the aircraft was crewed by squadron OC, Wg Cdr J M Birkin DSO, DFC, AFC, and Flt Lt Saunders. ML942 completed 91 operations and suffered two aborts with No 571 Sqn before it failed to return from a raid on Berlin on 5/6 January 1945. Flown on this occasion by Flg Offs F Henry and 'Blue' Stinson, 'D-Dog' was hit by flak during its bombing run. Henry managed to nurse it as far as the Belgian-French border, where it entered a spin and the crew were forced to bale out.

9

B Mk XXV KB462/CR-B of No 162 Sqn, Bourn, December 1944

This aircraft was assigned to No 162 Sqn at Bourn on 17 December.and was later assigned to No 627 Sqn at Woodhall Spa, who flew it until they disbanded on 1 October 1945 – the unit was renumbered No 109 Sqn on the same day. KB462 finished its career with this unit, being struck off charge on 22 October 1947.

10

B Mk XVI MM138/P3-A *Moncton Express III* of No 692 Sqn, No 8 Group (PFF), flown by Flt Lt Andy Lockhart DFC, RCAF, and Flt Lt Ralph Wood DFC, RCAF, Graveley, October 1944

The third, and last, aircraft to bear this name, MM138 was predominantly the mount of Flt Lts Andy Lockhart DFC, RCAF and F/L Ralph Wood DFC, RCAF during their tour of 50 operations, flown between 6 July and 3/4 November 1944. The first Moncton Express (P3-J) was very badly damaged by cannon fire whilst being flown by another crew. Lockhart and Wood used Moncton Express II (P3-A) for the first time on 8 September, when they flew her to Nuremburg at 29,000 ft laden down with a 'Cookie'. This aircraft was lost while they were on leave, and Moncton Express III made its debut on 29/30 September when they went to Karlsruhe. It was also the mount for their final sortie, which saw them visit Berlin for the 17th time.

11

B Mk IV Series II *Oboe* marker DK333/HS-F *Grim Reaper* of No 109 Sqn, No 8 Group (PFF), flown by Flg Offs Harry B Stephens and Frank R Ruskell DFC, Wyton, January 1943

On 27 January 1943 DK333 was one of three Mosquitoes to drop the first ground target indi-cators (250-lb marker bombs) in action. In 1944 Flg Offs Harry B Stephens and Frank Ruskell DFC flew DK333 during their tour, the latter leaving No 109 Sqn in April 1944 whilst the former was later killed in action. DK333 also served with Nos 105, 139 and 192 Sqns, before being struck off charge on 30 May 1945.

12

B Mk IV Series II DZ650/P3-L of No 692 Sqn, No 8 Group (PFF), Graveley, May 1944

B Mk IV Series II DZ650, whose bomb bay was strengthened and the bomb doors redesigned to carry a 4000-lb bomb, was delivered to No 692 Sqn (the first Mosquito unit to drop a 4000-lb bomb over Germany) at Bourn on 15 May 1944. P3-L flew its first operation on 28/29 May 1944, and was allocated to No 627 Sqn at Woodhall Spa on 27 July 1944, where it became AZ-Q. On 29 December 1944 DZ650 was one of eight Mosquitoes detailed to carry out 'Gardening' (minelaying) operations in the Elbe, but it was damaged beyond repair during a take-off crash at the start of this mission.

13

B Mk XVI ML963/8K-K, No 692 Sqn, flown by Flg Off R Oliver and Flt Sgt M Young, April 1945

Originally assigned to No 109 Sqn, ML963 was transferred to No 692 Sqn before finally arriving at No 571 Sqn on 12 April 1944 – 'K-King' performed the latter unit's premier sortie on 12/13 April. Between 20-24 March 1945, ML963 (now coded 'F-Freddie') flew six consecutive operations to Berlin. It was finally lost on a yet another flight to Berlin on 10/11 April (ML963's 87th mission) when it suffered an engine fire. Having firstly jettisoned their 4000-lb bomb, Flg Off Richard Oliver and Flt Sgt Max Young successfully baled out near the Elbe.

14

B Mk IV DZ383/? of No 138 Wing, 2nd TAF, Lasham, September 1944

This aircraft was known as 'the query' because it did not belong to any single unit within the three squadrons that comprised No 138 Wing, 2nd TAF, at Lasham, in Hampshire, in 1943-44. A Polish airman's first attempt to paint a question mark on DZ383 went awry as he got it the wrong way round on one side! On 17 September 1944, Flt Lt Vic A Hester of No 613 Sqn and cameraman Flg Off Ted Moore filmed firstly the attack on a barracks at Arnhem ahead of the Market Garden operation, then the actual airborne drop itself. During the Shellhaus raid on 21 March 1945, DZ383 was flown by Flg Off R E 'Bob' Kirkpatrick,an American pilot with No 21 Sqn, accompanied by cameraman Sgt R Hearne from No 4 FPU. Although the Mosquito was damaged by flak over Copenhagen, Kirkpatrick nursed 'the query' back to Norfolk, where he force-landed at the USAAF B-24 base at Rackheath, near Norwich.

15

FB VI MM404/SB-T of No 464 Sqn, RAAF, No 140 Wing, 2nd TAF, flown by Sqn Ldr Ian McRitchie, RAAF, and Flt Lt R W 'Sammy' Sampson, 18 February 1944

Flown on the Amiens Prison raid on 18 February 1944, MM404 was hit by flak and crash-landed by a badly wounded McRitchie at over 200 mph, near Poix. He was made PoW, but his navigator, 'Sammy' Sampson, was killed.

16
FB VI MM417/EG-T of No 487 Sqn, RNZAF, No 140 Wing, No 2 Group, 2nd TAF, late February 1944

This aircraft suffered flak damage whilst attacking a Noball site at Le Haye, west of Carentan, in France, on 26 March 1944, and was written off in the subsequent crash-landing at its Hunsdon base.

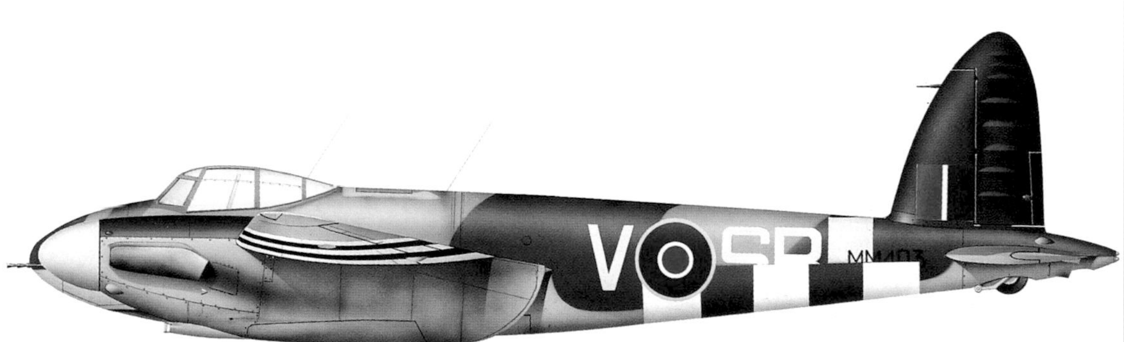

17
FB VI MM403/SB-V of No 464 Sqn, RAAF, No 140 Wing, No 2 Group, 2nd TAF, 18 February 1944

Also on the Amiens raid, this FB VI was crewed by Flt Lts Tom McPhee and Geoffrey W Atkins. It was one of five aircraft from the unit (along with the FB VI of Grp Capt Percy Pickard) that, between them, breached the walls of the main building and destroyed the guards' quarters at the eastern and western ends of the jail. MM403 was lost in action near Merville on 18 January 1945.

18
FB VI HX917/EG-E of No 487 Sqn, RNZAF, Hunsdon, July 1943

No 487 Sqn was part of the famous No 140 Wing which carried out a number of pin-point raids on German high-security targets in 1944-45. HX917 was lost on a night mission on 5 July 1944.

19
FB VI LR366/SY-L of No 613 Sqn, No 138 Wing, 2nd TAF, Lasham, January 1944

LR366 was assigned to this unit as on 10 January 1944, and was damaged on 5 February during a raid on a Noball site at Motteville. Assigned to No 107 Sqn on 27 July 1944 as OM-L, LR366 was lost on 17 September 1944 when 32 FB VIs of Nos 107 and 613 Sqn attacked the barracks at Arnhem ahead of the Market Garden airborne invasion.

20
FB VI HR405/NE-A, No 143 Sqn, Banff Strike Wing, flown by Flg Offs A V Randell and R R Rawlins

Part of an order for 500 FB VIs built by Standard Motors Ltd of Coventry between June 1943 and December 1944, little is known about the frontline service career of this aircraft.

21
FB VI LR347/T of No 248 Sqn, Banff Strike Wing, flown by Flt Lt Stanley G Nunn and Flg Off J M Carlin, 10 June 1944

This aircraft was used by Nunn and Carlin to attack Type VIIC U-boat U-821, commanded by Ober-leutnant Ulrich Knacfuss, off Ushant on 10 June 1944, the vessel eventually being sunk by Liberator EV943/K of No 206 Sqn. In July 1944 'T-Tommy' made a belly landing at Portreath after suffering flak damage which knocked out its port engine. The aircraft was repaired and later served with No 8 OTU, before being SoC in August 1946.

22
FB XVIII PZ468/QM-D of No 248 Sqn, North Coates, April 1945

This aircraft was one of five 'Tsetses' sent on detachment to Beaufighter-equipped No 254 Sqn at North Coates on 12 April 1945. Here, they were used primarily on operations off the coast of Holland against midget submarines and U-boats, with Spitfire Mk XIVs providing fighter cover. Two 'Tsetses' found five U-boats on the surface on 18 April 1945, and each got off just one round apiece before the submarines crash-dived.

23
FB VI RF610/DM-H, No 248 Sqn, Banff, April 1945

Built by Standard Motors Ltd of Coventry, this aircraft was delivered to No 248 Sqn at Banff in April 1945. Placed in storage after the unit disbanded in October 1946, RF610 was allocated to the French Government in April 1948, but this was rescinded and in July the aircraft was put to use at the Armament Practice Station at Acklington. In October 1949, after a further spell in storage with No 22 MU, the aircraft was flown to No 10 Ferry Unit at Abingdon for delivery (as '8114') to the Yugoslav Air Force on 10 September 1952.

1

Wg Cdr Hughie Edwards VC, DSO, DFC, OC No 105 Sqn at Marham in December 1942.
He is wearing standard RAF officer's Battle Dress over a white turtle-necked sweater. He has a C Type flying helmet, a Type G mask, US B-7 goggles and a Mark I life jacket. Edwards has lightweight gloves on his hands and is wearing 1939 Pattern issue boots.

2

Grp Capt Max Aitken DSO, DFC, OC Banff Strike Wing at Banff in October 1944.
Wearing Battle Dress 'tailor-made' of superfine material, Aitken has swapped his C Type helmet for a service dress cap. His remaining equipment is similar in style to that worn by Edwards, except for his oval-shaped goggles and steel-tipped shoes.

3
Wg Cdr John de Lacy Wooldridge DSO, DFC, DFM, OC No 105 Sqn at Marham in June 1943.
Again attired in regulation Battle Dress, Wooldridge is wearing a very battered service dress cap, which was obviously an old favourite from previous tours with Bomber Command.

4
Flt Lt R W 'Sammy' Sampson, RAAF, of No 464 Sqn, RAAF, at Hunsdon in February 1944.
Standing out in his matching RAAF dark blue service dress cap and Battle Dress (to which he has had an 'Australia' flash sewn onto the shoulder), Samp-son is seen holding his 'Chest' type parachute, the harness for which is worn over his life jacket. His goggles, helmet, oxygen mask and gloves are all standard 1943 issue, as are his boots.

A fitter carries out work on the starboard engine of DK300, a Mosquito B Mk IV Series II which had been delivered to No 109 Sqn at Stradishall, in Suffolk, on 21 July 1942 to have *Oboe* radar equipment installed. The following month No 109 Sqn moved to Wyton, where DK300 (and eight other B Mk IVs) was used for *Oboe* trials. Although this aircraft survived a lengthy combat tour, it broke up in flight over Pidley, which was then in Huntingdonshire (now Cambridgeshire), on 22 July 1944 whilst serving with No 1655 MTU

event of cloud cover over the target area. That same night two *Oboe* Mosquitoes dropped HE bombs through cloud from a height of 28,000 ft onto the nightfighter control room at Florennes airfield, in Belgium.

Oboe was the most accurate form of blind bombing used in World War 2, and it took its name from a radar pulse which sounded like a musical instrument. John C Sampson, a navigator in No 105 Sqn from the summer of 1944 to the end of the war, describes the system employed;

'The radar pulses operated on the range from two ground stations ("Cat" and "Mouse") in England across to the target (following the Normandy invasion, ground stations were located on the continent, thus increasing the effective range of the system). The signals went "line of sight", and did not follow the curvature of the earth, so the further the target, the higher one needed to be. The time on the bombing run was ten minutes on a slightly curved track, as it was a system based on range. The track to the target was extended backwards for a further five minutes. This was known as the "waiting point", but one did not actually wait there – it meant waiting for one's call-in signal. So, at zero minus 15 minutes, one turned onto the track to the target and switched on the *Oboe* receiver and listened out. When one heard the call-in signal we switched on the *Oboe* transmitter and began to receive signals from the ground station.

'The signals were heard by both pilot and navigator, and were used to track the aircraft over the target, If inside the correct line, dots were heard, and if outside the line, dashes, whilst a steady note indicated the target was on track. This signal was heard only by the navigator. When the release signal, which consisted of five dots and a two-second dash, was heard, the navigator released the markers or bombs.'

No 105 Sqn had flown its first *Oboe* operation on 13 July 1943 when

No 109 Sqn's Flt Lt Frank Griggs DFC, RAAF and Flt Lt A P 'Pat' O'Hara DFC*, DFM pose for the camera in front of their distinctively marked B Mk IV Mosquito at RAF Marham in 1943. This crew flew *Oboe* operations until January 1944 when Griggs was repatriated to Australia, O'Hara finishing his second tour (he and Griggs had earlier flown Stirlings together) flying with various pilots including Wg Cdr Peter Kleboe, OC 'A' Flight. On 25 October 1944, whilst marking Essen with red TIs, Kleboe and O'Hara's Mosquito was hit by a piece of flak that came through the windscreen of the aircraft just as the latter lent forward and pressed the lever to open the bomb bay doors. The scorching hot metal tore the left epaulette off O'Hara's battledress and peppered Kleboe's face with fragments of perspex, which left him practically blind. Despite his drastically reduced vision, the pilot got the Mosquito back to Little Staughton and landed it safely. Kleboe was later killed on the Shellhaus raid, flown on 21 March 1945

two B Mk IVs attempted to mark Cologne. In September the squadron began precision bombing of pin-point targets in western Germany.

The *Oboe* markers achieved such proficiency that Bennett was able to expand his Mosquito force, and in early 1943 No 8 Group began 'nuisance' raiding. By the summer this had become so effective that the Mosquitoes were now referred to as the Light Night Striking Force (LNSF, or, at Bennett's insistence, the *Fast* Night Striking Force). One of their greatest achievements came during the nine-day long (between 24/25 July and 2 August 1943) Operation *Gomorrah* (the 'Battle of Hamburg') – the PFF and LNSF flew 472 sorties for the loss of just 13 Mosquitoes. The first raid, which was led by both H_2S PFF aircraft and standard Mosquitoes, saw TIs used to mark targets for 728 bombers, which dropped 2284 tons of HE and incendiaries onto Hamburg in just 50 minutes, creating a fire-storm which rose to a height of 2 miles.

RAF losses were light due mainly to *Window*, which was being used for the first time – *Window* was the code-name for strips of black paper with aluminium foil stuck to one side, and cut to a length (30 cm by 1.5 cm) equivalent to half the wavelength of the Würzburg ground and *Lichtenstein* air intercept radars. When dropped by aircraft in bundles of 1000 at a time at one-minute intervals, *Window* reflected the radar waves and 'snowed' the tubes.

Yet another No 109 Sqn B Mk IV Series II to carry nose art, DK333 became one of the first Mosquitoes to drop ground target indicators (250 lb marker bombs) when it participated in a raid on 27 January 1943. This aircraft also served with No 192 Sqn, before finally being struck off charge on 30 May 1945

On 18/19 November 1943, 'spoof' raiding was first tried by No 139 Sqn, who used *Window* to give the impression that they were a large bomber force when in fact they were flying in just squadron strength – whilst this was occurring, the 'heavies' were en route to the real target. On 26 November three Mosquitoes from this unit flew ahead of the Main Force scattering *Window* on the approaches to Berlin, before returning to drop bombs. They also made feint attacks on other targets at distances of up to 50 miles away from the main stream in order to attract nightfighters away from the 'heavies'.

Late in November 1943 No 627 Sqn was formed at Oakington, near Cambridge, followed by No 692 Sqn, which became the fifth Mosquito unit within No 8 Group, at Gravely on 1 January 1944. The latter squadron had the dubious honour of being the first Mosquito unit to drop a 4000-lb bomb (known variously as a 'Blockbuster', 'Cookie' or 'Dangerous Dustbin' because of its shape) on a German target when DZ647 – one of a small number of modified B Mk IVs – released one during a raid on Düsseldorf on 23/24 February. Although the B Mk IV had a strengthened bomb bay and modified bomb bay doors, it was not entirely suitable for the job of carrying a 4000 'pounder'. Nevertheless, 'Cookies' continued to be carried in modified B Mk IVs until the B Mk XVI high-altitude Mosquito (with its bulged bomb bay and more powerful 1680 hp Merlin 72/76, or two 1710-hp 73/77engines, which gave the aircraft a top speed of 419 mph at 28,500 ft) became operational. No 692 Sqn debuted the B Mk XVI over Duisburg on 5/6 March 1944.

The winter of 1943-44 saw the start of Bomber Command's offensive against Berlin, masterminded by its C-in-C, Air Marshal Harris. Sixteen major raids were flown against the 'Big City' in quick succession, but the capital was too vast, and the weather often too bad, to allow effective results to be achieved. On 1/2 February 1944, No 139 Sqn, which had pioneered the use of Canadian-built Mosquitoes, and was now operating a mix of B Mk IVs, IXs, XVIs and XXs, used H_2S for the first time to mark the target during a raid on Berlin. H_2S provided a map-like image on a CRT (radar scope screen) which, in the Mosquito, was connected to a revolving scanner antennae housed in a bulbous nose radome. Targets had to be carefully selected using H_2S, with city areas sited on coastlines or estuaries being more easily picked out than land-locked targets because of the verifiable distinction between water and land on radar screens.

From 1944, H_2S-equipped B Mk IXs of No 139 Sqn frequently led operations or marked for other Mosquitoes, whilst *Oboe* Mk II-equipped B Mk IXs of Nos 109 and 105 Sqns spearheaded the main force bombing

A train of 4000-lb 'Cookie' bombs arrive at dispersal at Graveley for loading aboard B Mk XXVIs of No 692 Sqn. This unit was formed with B Mk IVs at the Cambridgeshire airfield on 1 January 1944, and flew its first LNSF operation on 1/2 February when three Mosquitoes were sent to bomb Berlin. By early 1944 suitably modified B Mk IVs were capable – just – of carrying a 4000-lb 'Blockbuster', although the outsized weapon had to be carefully 'squeezed' into the strengthened bomb bay, which also boasted redesigned bomb doors. No 692 Sqn had the distinction of being the first Mosquito unit to drop a 4000-lb bomb on Germany when DZ647 (a modified B Mk IV) took part in the Düsseldorf raid on the night of 23/24 February 1944. B Mk XVIs eventually replaced the modified B Mk IVs from June 1944 onwards, the former remaining in service until October 1945

As with the modified B Mk IV, No 692 Sqn also debuted the first 4000-lb bomb capable B Mk XVIs in combat when a small number participated in a raid on Duisburg on 5/6 March 1944 – 'Cookies' were dropped for the first time on Berlin on 13/14 April, again by No 692 Sqn. The B Mk XVI, with its bulged bomb bay and more powerful Merlin engines, was a much more acceptable 'Cookie carrier' than the 'interim' B Mk IV. This evocative photo shows B Mk XVI MM230 closing on the camera-ship at high altitude. This Mosquito, which had originally been built as a PR IX in November 1943, was retained by de Havilland for development work until struck of charge on 22 October 1946

raids. In the 12 months from January to December 1944, apart from No 692 Sqn, which was mentioned earlier in this chapter, five more Mosquito units joined No 8 Group. The first of these was No 571 Sqn, which formed at Downham Market on 7 April. A shortage of Mosquitoes initially meant that the unit had to operate at half-strength for a time. Although light on aircraft, the unit nevertheless participated in its first mission on the night of 13/14 April, when two crews from No 571 Sqn joined forces with six from No 692 Sqn in an attack on Berlin – each aircraft carried two 50-gallon drop tanks and a 4000-lb bomb.

On 1 August No 608 Sqn formed at Downham Market, and on 15 September No 128 Sqn stood up at Wyton and immediately joined the LNSF. On 25 October No 142 Sqn re-formed at Gransden Lodge, and that same night they flew their first operation when their only two B Mk XXVs were despatched to Cologne. On 18 December No 162 Sqn re-formed at Bourn with B Mk XXVs, and soon accompanied the veteran No 139 Sqn on target-marking duties – No 163 Sqn, the 11th, and final, Mosquito unit within No 8 Group, reformed at Wyton on 25 January 1945 on B Mk XXVs. Led by Wg Cdr (later Air Marshal) Ivor Broom DFC, the squadron flew its first LNSF operation just four days later when four Mosquitoes dropped *Window* at Mainz ahead of the PFF force.

Since the beginning of 1944, No 617 Sqn of 'Dam Buster' fame (led by Wg Cdr Leonard Cheshire VC, DSO*, DFC) had successfully employed the tactic of marking and destroying small industrial targets at night using flares dropped by a Lancaster in a shallow dive at low level. Obviously the Avro 'heavy' had limitations in this role, so Air Marshal the Hon Ralph Cochrane, urged on by Cheshire, gave the unit a Mosquito. No 617 Sqn's first sortie with the type occurred on 5/6 April 1944 when Wg Cdr Cheshire (along with navigator Flg Off Pat Kelly) marked an aircraft factory at Toulouse on his third pass with two red spot flares from a height of 800-1000 ft. He later used this aircraft (ML976/N) on 10/11 April to mark a signals depot at St Cyr during a dive from 5000 to 1000 ft.

These successes led to No 617 Sqn receiving four FB Mk VIs/XVIs, which were first used for marking the Paris-Juvisy marshalling yards on 18/19 April, along with three *Oboe* Mosquitoes of No 8 Group. A force comprising 202 Lancasters from No 5 Group (led by Cheshire himself) and a handful of Mosquitoes carried out a massed attack on the yards. The target area had been marked at each end with red spot-fires, and the Lancasters duly dropped their bombs between the TIs. As a result of the bombing being concentrated, the yards were put out of action and few French lives were lost – all but one Lancaster returned safely to base. Indeed, the railway yards were so badly damaged that they were only reopened in 1947. La Chapelle was marked on 20/21 April by three No 617 Sqn Mosquitoes, whilst Brunswick became the first German city to be targeted by the low level marking method on 22/23 April.

Sir Arthur Harris, who had sanctioned the release of the four Mosquitoes, said they could be retained by No 617 Sqn if Munich was hit heavily on the night of 24/25 April – in preparation for this long range operation, the quartet of aircraft moved to Manston, on the Kent coast. Once over the target the four Mosquitoes proved highly successful in completing their task, Cheshire diving from 12,000 to 3000 ft and then flying repeatedly over the city at little more than 700 ft, coming under fire for a whole 12 minutes before leaving the area. Sqn Ldr Dave Shannon dived from 15,000 to 4000 ft, but his markers hung up, whilst the fourth Mosquito got four spot flares away. Ninety per cent of the bombs fell in the right place, doing more damage in one night than had been achieved by Bomber Command and the Eighth Air Force combined in the preceding four years. Cheshire's contribution to the success of the raid was mentioned in his VC citation, issued on 8 September 1944.

In April 1944 No 627 Sqn was transferred from No 8 to No 5 Group at Woodhall Spa for specialised marking operations. The Lancaster pathfinder squadrons would identify the target areas on H_2S and then lay a concentrated carpet of flares, under which No 627 Sqn would locate and mark the precise aiming point in a shallow dive with 500-lb spot-fires. Under the direction of a 'Master of Ceremonies' in one of the pathfinder Lancasters, the target would then be destroyed by No 5 Group

Left and below
A 'Cookie' is slowly winched into the bulged bomb bay of a No 692 Sqn Mosquito in preparation for a raid on the 'Big City'. This aircraft was subsequently flown to Berlin by Canadians Flt Lts Andy Lockhart and Ralph Wood (navigator) – the pair completed 50 operations in Mosquitoes, including 18 trips to Berlin

Their 50-gallon underwing drop tanks clearly visible, a trio of No 128 Sqn B Mk XVIs taxy onto the runway at Wyton at the start of yet another sortie to Berlin. Mosquitoes flew so often to the 'Big City' that crews dubbed the mission the 'Berlin Express', with the different routes there and back being known as 'platforms one, two and three'. No 128 Sqn, which reformed as a Pathfinder unit within No 8 (PFF) Group on 15 September 1944, was initially issued with B Mk XXs before standardising on the B Mk XVI

heavy bombers. This group was now used exclusively in support of the bombing campaign against interdiction targets for Operation *Overlord*, as Flt L J R 'Benny' Goodman, a pilot with No 627 Sqn, recalls:

'The Americans were nervous about the gun battery at St Martin de Varreville, behind *Utah* beach. This presented a threat to Allied shipping approaching Normandy, and also to the troops landing on *Utah* beach. It was decided that No 5 Group would attack this precision target, so on the night of 28/29 May 1944, a force of 64 Lancasters, led by a flare force from Nos 83 and 97 Lancaster Pathfinder Sqns, and four Mosquitoes of No 627 Sqn, flew to St Martin de Varreville. The flare force identified the gun battery on their H_2S sets and laid a carpet of flares over thetarget. At Zero Hour minus five minutes, the Mosquitoes roared in at 2000 ft and identified the gun battery visually. The first pilot to see the target called "Tally Ho" on his VHF radio to warn his companions to keep out of the way, and then proceeded to dive at the gun, releasing red TIs at the appropriate point in the dive. His companions followed suit, making individual dives on the battery and creating a box of red TIs around it. The Master Bomber now called in the Main Force, with each aircraft carrying several 1000-lb armour-piercing bombs, and the target was obliterated.

'An American parachute force landed near St Martin de Varreville on D-Day, and an element of the 502nd Regiment made for the coastal battery. Their orders were to overrun the battery and to crush the garrison if necessary. Capt Frank Lilleyman, the first US soldier to land in Normandy on D-Day, reconnoitered the battery and discovered that it had

Already a veteran of an operational tour with No 692 Sqn, B Mk IV (Modified) DZ633 went on to see more action with No 627 Sqn following its arrival at Woodhall Spa on 12 August 1944. Just 19 days later the bomber was hit by flak over Rollencourt, and despite suffering considerable damage to both wings, its crew managed to reach Woodhall Spa. Having been repaired, DZ633 was struck again by flak on 17 September over the Boulogne area during a photo recce mission – one engine was hit and had to be feathered, but again the aircraft made it back to base. On 31 December 1944 DZ633 took part in the raid on the Gestapo HQ at Oslo and was duly hit again by a cannon shell over the target. Flt Lt Wallace 'Johnno' S Gaunt DFC* was struck by shell splinters in the thigh, and his pilot, Flt Lt Peter F Mallender DFC, gave him first aid prior to performing a ground loop landing at Peterhead. The aircraft was repaired for a third time and returned to operations on 12 February 1945 – it was finally struck off charge on 30 May 1945

A true combat veteran, B Mk XVI ML963 is seen wearing the markings of No 571 Sqn. Prior to being issued to this unit (who used it on their very first sortie on 12/13 April 1944 – a raid to Osnabruck), the bomber had seen service with Nos 109 and 692 Sqns. This classic Charles E Brown photo, taken during a test flight from Hatfield on 30 September 1944, shows the Mosquito immediately after major repair work had been carried out by the manufacturers to rectify severe flak damage sustained by the aircraft during an operation to Scholven on 6 July 1944 – its crew on this raid was Wt Off Russell Longworth and Plt Off Ken Davidson. This was the second time that ML963 had suffered combat damage, having earlier been hit by flak during a raid on Brunsbuttellkoog on 12 May – on this occasion repairs had commenced on 25 May and the aircraft returned to the squadron on 26 June. ML963 was reissued to No 571 Sqn for a second time on 18 October 1944, and on New Year's Day 1945 it was used by Flt Lt N J Griffiths and Flg Off W R Ball in the precision raids on railway tunnels in the Eiffel region during the Battle of the Bulge – their 4,000-lb delayed-action bomb des-troyed a tunnel at Bitburg. ML963 was lost during a raid on Berlin on 10/11 April 1945 following an engine fire, its crew, Flg Off Richard Oliver and Flt Sgt Max Young, successfully bailing out near the Elbe

been bombed out and abandoned as a result of the No 5 Group attack.'

Post-D-Day, No 5 Group Mosquitoes continued their marking of targets in France for the Main Force, while Bennett's LNSF in No 8 Group went after German cities. Canadians Flt Lts Andy Lockhart and Ralph Wood (the former's navigator) flew 50 operations in Mosquitoes with No 692 Sqn during this time and into 1945. Wood recalls that the 'daddy of them all' occurred on the night of 5/6 October1944 when six Mosquitoes from No 692 Sqn (five carried a 1000-lb mine and one a 1500-lb mine) and four from No 571 Sqn mined the Kiel Canal:

'We dropped our "vegetable" from a height of 100 ft. It was "wizard" flying at roof-top level over the villages and farm houses. The Canal was well defended by 97 light AA guns, balloons and 25 searchlights. One searchlight got us and a gun opened fire at our Mosquito from head-on when we were about 200 ft off the deck. It was rather alarming, but the gunners missed us. All of the Mosquitoes got back, although one pilot flew back with a dead navigator beside him for company. We really enjoyed ourselves, but we had the "twitch" before reaching the target.'

On 6/7 November, Bomber Command despatched 235 Lancasters to attack the Mittelland Canal at Gravenhorst – the target marking was carried out by seven Mosquitoes from No 627 Sqn. The latter eventually found the canal after great difficulty, whereupon Sqn Ldr F W Boyle, RAAF and Flt Lt L C E De Vigne dropped their marker with such a degree of accuracy that it fell into the water and was extinguished! Only 31 Lancasters bombed before the Master Bomber called for the raid to be abandoned. The 48 Mosquitoes despatched to Gelsenkirchen on a 'spoof' raid to draw German nightfighters away from both the Mittleland attack and a No 3 Group raid on Koblenz had better luck.

The Gelsenkirchen raid began as planned some five minutes ahead of the two main attacks at 19.25 hours. The city was still burning as a result of the afternoon raid by 738 RAF 'heavies', and from 25,000 ft, the Mosquitoes added their red and green TIs and HE to the fires. A few searchlights and only very light flak greeted the crews over the devastated city.

B Mk XVI '8K-R' of No 571 Sqn was flown from Oakington in 1944 by Flg Off H A 'Mike' Hooper DFC and Flt Sgt Alex Arbuckle DFM. Both men survived their tour (May to November 1944) and were duly posted to No 1655 MTU

Berlin was the most frequent target city for the LNSF. The Mosquitoes flew there so often (170 times, 36 of these on consecutive nights) that the raids were called the 'milk run' or, alternatively, the 'Berlin Express', and the different routes there and back were known as 'Platforms one, two and three'. A usual bomb load was 4000 lbs, and a typical trip to the 'snake's home' would see feint attacks made on a couple of cities enroute to the target, before *Window* was used to disrupt the enemy's radar nearer to Berlin itself. Flt Lts Andy Lockhart and Ralph Wood flew 18 operations to Berlin, the former recalling:

'Once over Berlin we were usually caught in a huge cone of searchlights that so blinded Andy that he couldn't read the instruments – "Are we upside down or not?" he'd ask. I'd look down at the bombs exploding below and assure him that we were rightside up! As the anti-aircraft crap seemed to surround us, Andy would throw our *Moncton Express* around the skies, trying to get out of the searchlights. On three occasions we lost an engine about now and had to limp home, one set of searchlights passing us on to another set, and so on, until they ran out of lights.

'Sometimes the boys were coned here and there, but no flak was shot up the beams, which indicated that enemy fighters were present. When over the target, we'd bomb and get out as fast as we could. This is when I'd sit

Another evocative Charles E Brown photograph of No 571 Sqn's ML963 – coded 'K-King' – taken on 30 September 1944 over Hatfield

in my seat, the blood draining out of my face and my stomach in tight knots. "Jesus, this could be it", I thought. And after tight moments like this I'd say, "Andy. Pass the beads". Once we dropped our wing tanks along with the "cookie" as the groundcrew had it wired up wrong. We were coned over the "Big City" but got out of it in four minutes, with only one hunk of flak in our wing. I hope my 18 visits to Berlin accomplished something. On our return trips we faced the terrors of flak and a new adversary in the form of the first jets rising into the skies over Germany.'

At first light on 2 January 1945, with the Battle of the Bulge still raging in the Ardennes, No 8 Group Mosquitoes were asked to fly one of the most remarkable daylight operations of the war. Bomber Command had to cut the railway supply lines through the Eifel region between the Rhine and the Ardennes, so while the 'heavies' bombed marshalling yards near Koblenz and Cologne, precision attacks on 14 railway tunnels in the target area were carried out by 17 Mosquitoes of Nos 128, 571 and 692 Sqns. Each aircraft carried a 4000-lb delayed-action bomb, which the crew skip-bombed into the mouths of the tunnels from a height of between 100 and 200 ft. PF411 (a No 128 Sqn B Mk XVI) crashed on take-off, killing the crew, whilst the remaining four Mosquitoes from this unit enjoyed mixed results. Six out of seven B Mk XVIs of No 692 Sqn bombed tunnels near Mayen, losing PF414 (and crewmen Flt Lt George Nairn and Sgt Danny Lunn) to light flak. It was left to the five crews from No 571 Sqn to cause the most damage, with one bomb dropped by B Mk XVI ML963/'K-King' (crewed by Flt Lt Norman J Griffiths and Flg Off W R Ball) destroying a tunnel at Bitburg.

With the war in Europe reaching a conclusion, the Mosquitoes were repeatedly called upon to mark for the bombers in daylight. One of the most dramatic marking operations of the war occurred on 14 March when a Mosquito from No 5 Group and eight *Oboe* Mosquitoes of Nos 105 and 109 Sqns set out to mark the Bielefeld and Arnsburg viaducts for fellow group Lancasters. Although the four Mosquitoes attempting to mark the latter target for No 9 Sqn failed in the attempt (resulting in no damage being caused to the viaduct) and three of the *Oboe* Mosquitoes were unable to mark the Bielefeld viaduct for No 617 Sqn, Flg Off G W Edwards of No 105 Sqn (in B Mk XVI MM191) succeeded in getting his markers on target. This resulted in more than 100 yards of the viaduct collapsing under the weight of the explosions – 28 of the 32 Lancasters despatched carried *Tallboys* and one from No 617 Sqn dropped the first 22,000-lb *Grand Slam* bomb.

The biggest No 8 Group Mosquito operation to Berlin took place on 21/22 March when 142 aircraft carried out two attacks for the loss of one aircraft. The group made their last daylight raid on 6 March when 48 Mosquitoes, led by *Oboe* leaders from No 109 Sqn, bombed Wesel. The final attack on Berlin by Mosquitoes came on 20/21 April when 76 aircraft completed six raids. On 25 April, 359 Lancasters and 16 Mosquitoes (including eight *Oboe* markers) went to bomb Hitler's 'Eagle's Nest' chalet and SS barracks at Berchtesgaden, but the Alps blocked all radar signals and none of the *Oboe* aircraft were able to bomb.

On 25/26 April 12 Mosquitoes dropped leaflets over PoW camps in Germany telling Allied prisoners that the end of the war was imminent, followed three days later by the commencement of Operation *Manna* –

B Mk IX LR503 set a Bomber Command record for the Mosquito by completing 213 operational sorties (the aircraft flew firstly with No 109 Sqn, before being passed onto No 105 Sqn) between 1943-45. This photo, taken at Bourn, in Cambridgeshire, soon after the bomber had returned from its 203rd mission, shows the aircrew watching the aircraft's scoreboard being brought up to date

the air-dropping of food to the starving Dutch population in German-occupied Holland. *Oboe* Mosquitoes were extensively employed marking drop zones for RAF and USAAF heavy bombers, whose bomb bays were filled with provisions instead of high explosives

It was feared that Germany might stage a last stand in Norway when troopships assembled at Kiel, so, on the night of 2/3 May, three raids by 142 Mosquitoes from No 8 Group and 37 Mosquitoes of No 100 Group were made. This was Bomber Command's final operation of the war.

During January-May 1945 the LNSF flew almost 4000 sorties, whilst the total war tally for Mosquitoes of No 8 Group stood at 28,215 sorties by VE-Day. Despite this huge number, the Mosquito force suffered the lowest losses in Bomber Command – 108 aircraft, or 1 loss per 2800 sorties, while 88 more aircraft were damaged beyond repair. Well over two-thirds of these sorties were flown on nights when the Main Force was grounded.

By the spring of 1945 Bomber Command HQ had decided that LR503 had earned a break from the frontline, so Flt Lt Maurice Briggs DSO, DFC, DFM (right) and navigator Flg Off John Baker DFC* (themselves veterans of 107 sorties) flew the Mosquito to Canada for a goodwill tour. As can be seen from this shot, taken on 23 April 1945, the bomber's white dope bomb tally was resprayed in a darker shade following the fitment of a new glazed nose fairing – note that Hitler's uniform, the bomb above his head and the tail of the wasp also appear to have been touched up in a darker colour. Both Briggs and Baker were killed when LR503 inexplicably crashed at Calgary Airport during a flying display on 10 May 1945

2nd TAF

On 1 June 1943, No 2 Group's 11 Norfolk-based Boston, Ventura and Mitchell squadrons were used to form the 2nd Tactical Air Force under the command of AVM Basil Embry. Its brief was simple – help prepare the way for the invasion of the continent, which was planned for the summer of 1944. Embry, whose command immediately began moving to airfields in Hampshire so as to be nearer to the invasion coastline, wanted Mosquito FB VIs, but the 'wooden wonder' was in short supply, so priority was given to the re-equipment of the three units flying Lockheed's obsolescent Ventura – Nos 21, 464 (RAAF) and 487 (RNZAF) Sqns.

Flt Lt Charles Patterson, who at this time was flying the Film Unit's Mosquito B Mk IV DZ414 within the newly-created 2nd TAF, explains;

'The Ventura must have been quite the worst aircraft ever sent into operation. Not only was it extremely limited from an operational standpoint, but it was also an absolute devil to fly, being heavy, cumbersome and unmanoeuvrable. Due to the dynamic drive and determination of Basil Embry, all three Ventura squadrons were re-equipped with Mosquito FB VI fighter-bombers.'

The FB VI was a day and night fighter-bomber, intruder and long range fighter, powered by two 1460 hp Merlin 21/23s or two 1635 hp Merlin 25s. The prototype flew for the first time on 1 June 1942, and production aircraft began rolling out the de Havilland factory in February 1943. Ultimately, some 2289 (almost a third of the total Mosquito production) would be built. Charles Patterson again:

'A conversion flight was formed at Sculthorpe under Sqn Ldr George Parry DSO, DFC*, and I was his deputy. We converted these three-squadrons to Mosquitoes in about six weeks (Nos 464 and 487 Sqns

The Mosquito FB VI was used exclusively by the six fighter-bomber squadrons of Nos 138 and 140 Wings of the 2nd Tactical Air Force. FB VI HX917/EG-E of No 487 Sqn, RNZAF, No 140 Wing, is seen here taxying out at the start of a sortie from its Hunsdon base in July 1943. Mosquito day bombers were camouflaged in dark green/light grey upper surfaces and light grey undersurfaces, with duck egg blue spinners and fuselage band. This scheme was modelled on Fighter Command colours of the same period in an effort to make attacking Luftwaffe fighter pilots believe the FB VIs were actually armed fighter variants of the Mosquito. Sadly, this ruse did not work so well at night, and HX917 was lost on a nocturnal intruder raid over France on 5 July 1944

received their first FB VIs in August, and No 21 Sqn got theirs inSeptember, all three units going on to form No 140 Wing), giving dual all the time until they flew their first operation, which was a comparatively easy one.'

On Sunday, 3 October 1943, every bomber squadron in No 2 Group was allocated one in a series of transformer stations between Paris and Brittany which were to be attacked from low level. Nos 487 and 464 Sqn's targets were the power-stations at Pont Chateau and Mur de Bretange. Patterson continues:

This still was taken from the cine camera film shot from Wg Cdr Bob Iredale's No 464 Sqn FB VI MM412/SB-F during Operation *Jericho* – the precision attack on Amiens Prison on 18 February 1944. One of the most famous missions of the war, the raid saw the prison walls breached by 12 FB VIs from Nos 464, RAAF, and 487, RNZAF, Sqns. This action allowed many of the 700 inmates to escape, although most were latter recaptured. The aircraft trailing in MM412's wake is MM402/SB-A, flown by Sqn Ldr W R C Sugden, and his navigator Flg Off A H Bridger. The latter FB VI was lost on operations on 21 March 1944, but MM412 survived a further tour of combat with No 487 Sqn and time with No 13 OTU and No 1 Overseas Ferry Unit, before eventually being sold to the Yugoslav Air Force in April 1952

'I was to film the attack by No 487 Sqn. We all went down to Exeter. Basil Embry decided to go on the trip himself and fly somewhere towards the rear of No 464 Sqn. He took his navigator, David Atcherley, who was the twin brother of the famous Wg Cdr D F W 'Batchie' Atcherley of Fighter Command. His SASO (Senior Air Staff Officer) at No 2 Group, Grp Capt Percy Pickard, went too.

'All went smoothly, with the normal low level approach to the coast and then the shallow dive onto the first target. I carried on alone as usual, having to do my own map reading. As I came over the brow of a hill, my second target became clearly visible on my starboard wingtip, and at this point I got over confident – something that I had never previously allowed myself to become, because it usually had fatal results. Having flown past the target and alerted the area to my presence, I did a big sweep round in full view of any gunners and came in and attacked. I noticed that the target was quite undamaged – obviously No 484 Sqn had missed it altogether. I dropped my bombs.

'Then there was a tremendous bang in the cockpit, followed by a near-instantaneous cloud of blue smoke – I had just had my first experience of my aircraft being properly hit in a key area by a 20 mm cannon shell. My immediate reaction was to test the controls, and soon I realised that the aircraft was flying quite normally. We got clear of the target area and I began to feel a bit of a sting in my back – that was all. I was suddenly aware of the red face of the film cameraman (who had been in the nose adjusting his equipment) looking in bewilderment at me through the smoke. I said, "Don't just sit there gawping. Get back into your seat and get your map out and try and find out where we're supposed to be going. What are you looking like that for? The aircraft's perfectly all right".

'He pointed, and I turned round and had a quick look. The whole of the back of the cockpit had gone! A cap of mine which I always left behind my seat was in shreds. The radio and *Gee* set had been smashed too. I had been saved by the armour-plated seat, which had taken the blast, and the sting in my back was the result of a few small bits of shrapnel that had penetrated the plating. We carried on, with a bit of roaring noise from the

The graphic results of the precision attack on Amiens Prison – both the northern and southern perimeter walls were breached. The attackers came in from the north, so it must be assumed that the southern breach, to the left of the main gate, was caused by a bomb that skidded through the prison after being dropped from the east or the north. Both Plt Off D R Fowler of No 487 Sqn, flying HX974/EG-J, and Sqn Ldr Ian McRitchie of No 464 Sqn, in MM404/SB-T, have since claimed the same hole!

wind. Because I was flying a Mosquito B Mk IV, I had enough petrol to head on back to Norfolk, so I had returned to base with the film long before any of the others. My navigator and I went to tea, but we had great difficulty getting served our bacon and eggs because the WAAFs who manned the canteen said we couldn't have been in operations because nobody was back yet. I had to take off my battledress jacket and let the girl inspect the blood on my shirt in order to convince her!

'During these first few weeks after the wing had converted from Venturas to Mosquitoes, there were several botched up and aborted raids due to the fact that none of the experience gained by Nos 105 and 139 Sqns during their splendid months of 1942-43 was available, or used. Many of the losses suffered during those first weeks could have been completely avoided. They made all the same mistakes that we had done two years before.

'One more trip took place to try and rectify these problems. No 487 Sqn was sent out under a wing commander to do a low level daylight attack on an oil refinery on the River Loire, near St Nazaire. I would hopefully bring back film of an oil refinery blazing – splendid stuff for the newsreel. I took my own route, arrived down at the target, and looked across the Loire to find the refinery absolutely untouched. I went straight across and attacked it – we had a rear facing camera which confirmed I had indeed hit it. No 487 Sqn had never seen the target at all, and when Basil Embry saw the film and realised what had happened, he was very angry indeed. I was promoted to squadron leader and became a flight commander in No 487 Sqn.'

More Mosquito units were allocated to 2nd TAF in late 1943, with No 613 'City of Manchester' Sqn swapping Mustang Is for FB VIs at Lasham in October. No 305 'Polish' Sqn followed suit in December, trading in its Mitchell IIs for FB VIs and joining No 613 Sqn at the Hampshire base. On the last day of 1943, Nos 21, 464 and 487 Sqns took off from Sculthorpe for the last time, bombed Le Ploy, in France, and landed back at their new base at Hunsdon. On 1 February 1944, No 107 Sqn replaced

Sqn Ldr Ian McRitchie DFC, RAAF (left) and Flt Lt R W 'Sammy' Sampson of No 464 Sqn pose by their Mosquito, MM404/SB-T. This aircraft was hit by flak during *Jericho*, forcing a badly wounded McRitchie (he had 26 separate shrapnel wounds) to crash-land his shattered FB VI near Poix. Sampson did not survive the crash

its Bostons with Mosquito FB VIs and moved to Lasham. On 14 February No 226 Sqn also moved south to Hartford Bridge, although this unit retained its Mitchell II/IIIs until war's end.

The Mosquito FB VI boasted the same armament as the fighter version, but had the additional capability of being able to carry two 500-lb bombs in the rear half of the bomb bay – the forward half was taken up with cannon breeches. Wing racks were fitted to carry two 50-gallon drop tanks or a further two 500-lb bombs. In all, crews could carry out a round trip of 1000 miles carrying 4000 rounds of .303 ammunition, 1000 rounds of cannon shell and 2000 lbs of bombs, and still be able to cruise at between 255-325 mph.

During January-February 1944 the Mosquito FB VI units were kept busy destroying V1 flying-bomb launch sites in the Pas de Calais. No 613 Sqn pilot Ron Smith remembers the *Noball* or *Crossbow* operations, as they were code-named:

'The method of attack was to fly out at low level to the target area in loose formation in boxes of four or five aircraft, pull up to 3500 ft, peel off individually, dive down steeply to 1500 ft, release your four 500-lb bombs and return to base at low level. Our aircraft carried no bomb sights, so bombs were dropped at the crew's judgement. Most used the position of the target vis-a-vis the gunsight to decide when to release – taking into account the speed of the aircraft and the angle of the dive. It was simply a matter of practice and experience, and the end results were generally satisfactory. These targets were usually heavily defended by light ack-ack, and losses were experienced as well as numerous aircraft damaged.'

No 487 Sqn's Plt Offs Maxwell N Sparks (left) and Arthur C Dunlop (navigator) crewed HX982/EG-T during *Jericho*. Their FB VI also flew with Nos 613, 464 and 21 Sqns during its brief operational life. It was finally written off by a crew from the latter unit at Gravesend on 18 April 1944

No 487 Sqn crews who took part in the Amiens raid are interviewed by the BBC. Top, from left to right, Plt Off D R 'Bob' Fowler (pilot of HX974/EG-J), Plt Off M Barriball, Plt Off M L S Darrall (pilot of HX909/EG-C). Bottom, from left to right, Robin Miller, New Zealand War Correspondent, Plt Off Max Sparks (pilot of HX982/EG-T), David Bernard (BBC) and Plt Off F Stevenson (Darrall's navigator for the operation)

On average, Mosquito units destroyed one *Crossbow* site for each 39.8 tons of bombs dropped, compared with an average of 165.4 tons for the B-17, 182 tons for the Mitchell and 219 tons for the B-26. On occasion, 2nd TAF Mosquitoes were assisted in their attacks against *Noball* sites by two PFF Mosquitoes fitted with *Oboe*, with fighter escort provided by Spitfires. However, this technique meant that they had to fly in tight formation – straight and level – for ten minutes until bomb release, which made them easy targets for flak gunners!

AND THE WALLS CAME TUMBLING DOWN

Two notable pin-point raids were carried out in early 1944, the first of these being Operation *Jericho*, which targeted Amiens Prison. Over 700 French prisoners were known to be incarcerated inside this facility, and British Intelligence had discovered that some of the inmates were to be executed by the Germans on 19 February. 2nd TAF was therefore instructed to attack the prison 24 hours prior to the executions taking place. This task fell to No 140 Wing's Nos 487 and 464 Sqns, who were led on the raid by Grp Capt Percy Pickard and his navigator, Flt Lt 'Pete' Broadley, in the latter squadron's 'F-Freddie' (SB-F). The Mosquitoes took off from Hunsdon in terrible weather, each aircraft carrying 11-second delayed-fuse bombs to breach the prison's 20 ft high and 3 ft thick walls – it was also calculated that the concussion from the detonations would open the cell doors to give most of the prisoners a chance to escape. If Nos 487 and 464 Sqns failed in their mission, then FB VIs of No 21 Sqn, led by Wg Cdr I G 'Daddy' Dale, had orders to destroy the target. By the time the formation crossed the French coast, seven FB VIs and one of the three Typhoon squadrons sent to escort

FB VIs 'T', 'V' and 'D' of No 487 Sqn were photographed on 29 February 1944 each carrying two 500-lb bombs beneath their wings. None of these aircraft had participated in the Amiens prison raid, staged earlier that month

This close up shot shows MM417/ EG-T as featured in the three-ship formation seen on the previous page. This aircraft was written off on 26 March 1944 after suffering a heavy landing at Hunsdon as a result of flak damage inflicted over the Les Hayes V1 site

the Mosquitoes had aborted.

At precisely 12.01 pm, with the guards sat down to eat their lunch, bombs from 11 Mosquitoes hit the prison. The first bomb blew in almost all the doors and breached one of the outer walls. Flt Lt Tony Wickham, flying DZ414 (the FPU B Mk IV), made three passes over the burning prison to allow Plt Off Leigh Howard to film the flight of some 255 of the 700 prisoners held captive – 182 of them were later recaptured, whilst some of the 37 prisoners who died during the raid were machine-gunned to death by the sentries. Fifty German guards also died. Almost immediately after leaving the target 'F-Freddie' was shot down by a Fw 190 of II./JG 26, carrying Pickard and Broadley to their deaths, whilst No 464 Sqn's Sqn Ldr Ian McRitchie, RAAF, had his Mosquito peppered with flak. Despite being wounded in 26 places, the Australian pilot managed to crash-land his stricken FB VI near Poix, but his navigator, Flt Lt R W 'Sammy' Sampson, did not survive.

The second precision raid was carried out on 11 April by six FB VIs of No 613 Sqn against the five-storey, 95-ft high, Kunstzaal Kleizkamp Art Gallery in The Hague, which had been occupied by the Gestapo and used to house the Dutch Central Population Registry, as well as duplicates of all legally issued Dutch personal identity papers. The unit's OC, Wg Cdr R N Bateson DFC, led the operation in FB VI LR355, whilst his 'number two' in the second pair was Flt Lt Ron Smith in HP927:

'I was completely occupied by both flying the aircraft at very low level in formation and listening to my navigator, Flg Off John Hepworth, on what landmark to expect next. The way in was deliberately flown in a roundabout fashion in order to confuse the enemy in respect to our objective, and thus achieve maximum surprise. The first pair, led by the CO, had 30-second delayed action HE bombs, so we in the second pair, led by Sqn Ldr Charles Newman and Flt Lt F G Trevers, had to circle Lake Gouda in order to burn up all the exposed paper work released by the initial explosions. The third pair, led by Flt Lt Vic Hester and Flg Off R Birkett, finished off the mission by dropping HE and incendiary bombs.

'My final recollection is of coming out over playing fields filled with footballers, before crossing the coast north of the city and being escorted home by waiting Spitfires. For his leadership of this operation, Wg Cdr Bateson (who put his bombs literally through the front door!) was awarded the DSO and received the Dutch Flying Cross from Prince Bernhard of The Netherlands.'

The building was destroyed, as were the majority of the identity

Flt Lts Tony Wickham DFC (left) and B T 'Banger' Good, No 21 'City Of Norwich' Sqn's Armaments Officer, pose for the *Illustrated London News* photographer at Thorney Island on 19 December 1944 in front of FB VI 'Kay'. Wickham had participated in the 30 January 1943 daylight raid on Berlin, and went on to serve in No 618 Sqn on the *Highball* project, before being posted to No 21 Sqn, along with his navigator, Plt Off W E D Makin, on 8 September 1944. On 18 February 1944, Wickham flew the FPU's B IV DZ414 on the Amiens raid, making three passes over the burning prison so that his cameraman, Plt Off Leigh Howard, could film the flight of some 255 of the 700 prisoners held captive

papers. However, 61 civilians were killed, 24 seriously injured and 43 slightly injured. An Air Ministry bulletin later described the raid as 'probably the most brilliant feat of low-level precision bombing of the war'. During April-May FB VIs of 2nd TAF continued to hit German targets in France and the Low Countries in the build up to D-Day. Ron Smith adds:

'On the night of the D-Day landings, and for many nights afterwards, our chief role was patrolling over, and behind, enemy lines, attacking troop movements and anything in the way of enemy activity on the ground. Our mode of entry and exit was via the sea corridor between Alderney and the Cherbourg Peninsular, entering France at Granville and then making our way to the "Tennis Court", which was our patrol area. During the period 5 June to 11 July, John and I completed 17 operational sorties, all at night. In June these sorties were all in the Normandy area, attacking roads, bridges, marshalling yards and any lights or movements seen. Sometimes we would rendezvous with Mitchells, who would drop flares for us in order to improve target visibility.'

No 613 'City of Manchester' Sqn flew its first Mosquito operation from Hartford Bridge on 31 December 1943, attacking a V1 site in northern France. On 11 April 1944 the unit sent six FB VIs (led by Wg Cdr R N 'Pin Point' Bateson) to destroy the Kunstzaal Kleizkamp, a five-storey, 90-ft high, central registry building in The Hague which contained Gestapo records of the Dutch Resistance. This shot shows the immediate aftermath of the attack as seen out the rear of a fleeing FB VI

Each navigational log told a story. E S Gates of No 613 Sqn recalls:

'That pitch black night when, unfavourably placed, we dived steeply to attack a light and saw the dark silhouettes of trees rush past us on our starboard side as we abruptly climbed, a split-second away from oblivion. Then there was that occasion when, working as an intruder pair, Frankie Reede dropped a flare as we took up a favourable position to attack the target. Naked under the yellow light, and near blinded by its brilliance, we were engulfed by a tangled trellis of coloured tracer shells. Identifying nothing, and with the instincts of self-preservation uppermost in our minds, we dived away into the blackness beyond the flare.'

Until suitable airstrips could be made ready, the Mosquito wings flew operations from Thorney Island and Lasham. During this time some spectacular pinpoint daylight raids against specific buildings were flown. For example, on Bastille Day (14 July 1944) a large German Army barracks at Bonneuil Matours, near Poitiers, was attacked by 18 FB VIs of Nos 21, 487 and 464 Sqns. The Mosquitoes dropped nine tons of bombs (fused for 25 seconds' delay) in a series of shallow dives, destroying six buildings inside a rectangle of just 170 ft by 100ft – at least 150 soldiers were killed. On 1 August a follow up raid involving 24 Mosquito FB.VIs of Nos 487 and 21 Sqns, escorted by Mustangs, was made on the Caserne des Dunes barracks at Potiers, where about 2000 Germans were billeted. On 2 August, 23 FB VIs of Nos 107 and 305 Sqns attacked both the SS police HQ at Chateau de Fou, south of Chatellerault, and Chateau Maulny, which housed a school for saboteurs. No 613 Sqn, meanwhile, bombed a chateau in Normandy which was serving as a rest home for German submariners.

Armourers fit a 250-lb bomb to the wing of FB VI LR355/'H' of No 613 Sqn. This aircraft was still serving with the unit when it was written off in a crash-landing following an engine failure on 1 August 1944

FB VI LR366 of No 613 Sqn is rearmed and refuelled on a damp dispersal at Lasham on 7 February 1944. This aircraft went on to serve with No 107 Sqn later in the year, but was lost over Arnhem on 17 September 1944 – the opening day of Operation *Market Garden*. LR366 was hit by flak, caught fire and crashed near to the enemy position it had been attacking

A line up of No 464 Sqn FB VIs at Thorney Island in mid-1944. During April-May of that year Mosquitoes of 2nd TAF continued their bombing of targets in France and the Low Countries as part of the build up to D-Day. In June, sorties were flown exclusively over the Normandy area against roads, bridges, marshalling yards and any vehicles seen on the move

On 19 August 14 FB VI crews from No 613 Sqn were led by Sqn Ldr Charles Newman on a daring low level attack on a school building at Egletons, 50 miles south-east of Limoges, which British Intelligence believed was in use as an SS barracks. As usual, AVM Basil Embry and Grp Capt Bower went along to observe the squadron in action. Fourteen of the Mosquitoes located and bombed the target, scoring at least 20 direct hits which all but destroyed the school. One FB VI was struck in the starboard engine by flak over the target area and had to crash-land in France, but the crew returned to the squadron just five days later.

On 25/26 August No 138 Wing took part in all-out attacks in the Rouen area against troop concentrations and convoys of vehicles that were attempting to retreat across the Seine. Sorties continued on the night of 30 August against railways in the Saarbourg and Strassburg areas, followed 24 hours later by a raid on a huge petrol dump at Nomency, near Nancy. Twelve FB VIs of No 464 Sqn also attacked a dozen petrol trains near Chagney, their strafing and bombing runs at heights of between 20 to 200 ft causing widespread destruction.

On 17 September, as part of Operation *Market Garden* (the airborne

FB VI LR356/YH-Y (flown by Sqn Ldr Tony Carlisle) of No 21 Sqn is seen in planform from a second Mosquito at 20,000 ft over a *Noball* target in 1944. Whilst operating as part of No 140 Wing, 2nd TAF, this unit gained a reputation for pin-point bombing raids during 1944/45. On 6 February 1945 the squadron moved to Rosiéres-en-Santerre, in France, this airfield being the first in a series of continental bases used by the unit until war's end. LR356 completed two tours with No 21 Sqn, in between which was sandwiched a spell with No 613 Sqn. Returned to the latter unit after completing its second tour with No 21 Sqn, LR356 was lost on a night intruder mission over north-west Germany on 2 February 1945

invasion of Holland), 32 FB VIs from Nos 107 and 613 Sqns within No 138 Wing attacked the barracks at Arnhem, while No 21 Sqn bombed three school buildings in the centre of Nijmegen which were being used by the German garrison.

By November 1944 No 138 Wing's Nos 107, 305 and 613 Sqns had finally arrived in France to be based at Epinoy, near Cambrai. Meanwhile, Nos 21, 464 and 487 Sqns initially remained behind at Thorney Island, but in December the Australian and New Zealand units both sent advance detachments to Rosiäres-en-Santerre, in France, and by February 1945 all three squadrons were permanently based there.

By this stage of the war the enemy was being bombed both day and night. Nocturnal FB VIs also reaped a rich harvest of enemy aircraft, and continued to harrass troop movements behind the German thrust in the Ardennes, as well as flying close support sorties over the frontline. The Luftwaffe was powerless to stop their inexorable advance westwards, and even Operation *Bodenplatte* (which saw some 850+ fighters attack 27 airfields in northern France, Belgium and southern Holland early on New Year's Day) failed to halt the Allies.

Throughout January-March 1945, Nos 138 and 140 Wings, along with all the other Allied tactical units, continued the offensive on most nights by attacking German road and rail transport when possible, and bombing rail junctions using *Gee* when bad weather prevented visual sightings. The Mosquito coped well with the upturn in operations, as Flt Lt Eric Atkins (a pilot with No 305 'Polish' Sqn) remembers:

'Being small and light, the Mosquito could fall foul to bad weather. On the other hand, in emergency conditions, when caught in flak or searchlights, or when being attacked by enemy aircraft, it could be flung around the sky in almost impossible manoeuvres. The Mosquito responded to the controls like a thoroughbred racehorse, with speed, precision and a sixth sense of judgement linked to that of the pilot. I have also known the

In July-August 1944, FB VIs of 2nd TAF were called upon to make three pinpoint raids against barracks occupied by the 158th Security Regiment near the town of Poitiers, in France, after they had massacred captured Maquis and SAS troops at a site nearby. On Bastille Day, 14 July 1944, Hurricane ace Grp Capt Peter Wykeham-Barnes DSO*, DFC (pictured) led Nos 487 and 464 Sqns in an attack by 18 FB VIs on six buildings inside a rectangle just 170 ft x 100 ft at Bonneuil Matours, near Poitiers. The Mosquitoes destroyed the barracks with nine tons of bombs, dropped in shallow dives

On 30 July 1944 the Caserne des Dunes barracks at Poitiers was destroyed by Mosquitoes, and on 2 August the survivors of the notorious 158th Security Regiment – now billeted in the Chateau de Fou (pictured), an SS police HQ south of Chatellerault – were killed when the barracks was bombed by 23 FB VIs drawn from Nos 107 and 305 Sqns. It is estimated that 80 per cent of the regiment were killed as a result of the three separate raids

FB VI to turn in such a tight circle at night, in order to get away from searchlights and flak, that it virtually "disappeared up its own orifice".

'A Mosquito could fly well on one engine, providing you had the speed and height to gain level flight over a long distance. Many a Mosquito pilot flew back from Germany on one engine, but the landing could be tricky, and you never knew whether the other engine would overheat and pack up! A Mosquito would also do a safe belly landing, providing you remembered to come in without any undercarriage and flaps – the latter would invariably cause it to turn over. I landed at night on a grass 'drome at Epinoy, France, with no undercarriage, no flaps and a bomb aboard! The only annoying thing was that the ambulance and MO took over half an hour to reach us – they were waiting to see whether the bomb went off! The aircraft had only minor damage and was soon returned to service again. Other Mosquitoes landed with half a wing missing.

On 19 August 1944, 15 FB VIs of No 613 Sqn (led by Sqn Ldr Charles Newman) attacked a Gestapo HQ housed in a former school building at Egeltons, some 50 miles south-east of Limoges – intelligence on the site also indicated that the school was being used as a barracks for SS troops. The Mosquitoes located the target and bombed from low level, scoring at least 20 direct hits which left the building almost completely destroyed

'Despite its wooden construction the Mosquito had strength and endurance, and was easier to repair – you simply spliced another wing on! The speed of the Mosquito also meant that the operational time was less (unless you were "Ranging"), and the turn-around time was such that when German light vehicles were piled up around Rouen, an all-night attack was called. We did three operations in one night, landing, refuelling, rearming and away again – a dusk to dawn hat-trick!'

On 22 February 1945 Mosquito squadrons participated in Operation *Clarion* – a maximum daylight effort to deliver the *coup de grace* to the German transport system. Altogether, some 9000 Allied aircraft were involved in attacks on enemy railway stations, trains and engines, cross roads, bridges, ships and barges on canals and rivers, stores and other targets. P D Morris, a pilot with No 613 Sqn, recalls:

'The area given to Ron Parfitt (my navigator) and I to patrol was the very north of Germany up in Schleswig Holstein, near the Danish border. Our job was to patrol a large area and bomb, machine gun and cannon any enemy transport or personnel we spotted. After being able to cause a little havoc on various targets, the time came for us to make our way home. As we flew at low-level over fields separated by dykes that were at much the same height as us, a German soldier appeared at the top of a dyke some 300 yards ahead of us and proceeded to fire his gun in our direction. I was armed with both four machine guns and four cannon, and I took careful aim and pulled both triggers. My guns remained completely silent! However, I was determined to frighten him badly, so I passed over him at a few feet and saw him fall flat on his face. Once past the soldier I tried the guns again, and they fired perfectly!'

Clarion was to be the last time that the Mosquitoes operated in daylight in such numbers – Nos 138 and 140 Wings lost nine FB VIs, and many more were damaged.

No 613 Sqn's AC1 Phillip Beck and LAC E Kerslake – the 'boys with the gen' – refill FB VI 'W's' oxygen tanks in preparation for a raid on Berlin

B Mk IV DZ383/? was used by the FPU within No 138 Wing, 2nd TAF. The nose of the bomber was modified so as to be mostly made of perspex or glass panels, which allowed the cameraman to squat and shoot his cine films from virtually any angle. A 400f reel camera, fixed to shoot straight ahead, was also fitted into the aircraft. It was aimed by the pilot through the use of a simple gunsight installed in the cockpit. On 17 September 1944, DZ383 was flown by Flt Lt Vic A Hester (and cameraman Ted Moore) of No 613 Sqn during an attack on a barracks at Arnhem ahead of the *Market Garden* operation. After dropping its bomb, the B Mk IV was used as a photographic mount to capture the airborne assault on film

FB VIs 'B' and 'H' of No 613 Sqn are seen at A75/Cambrai-Epinoy, in France, in late 1944. The squadron had moved here, together with Nos 107 and 305 Sqns within No 138 Wing, in November 1944 in order to be closer to the frontline for their harrassing missions against German units retreating further eastwards

ABOVE THE WAVES

In autumn 1943 No 618 Sqn had detached five crews to the Beaufighter Mk X-equipped No 248 Sqn at Predannack to operate Mk XVIII 'Tsetse' Mosquitoes – so named because of the 57 mm Molins automatic weapon installed in the nose of the aircraft in place of the standard quartet of 20 mm cannon. Fitted primarily for use against surfaced U-boats, the gun was fed armour-plated HE 6-lb shells, capped with tracer, from an arc-shaped magazine that could hold 24 rounds. Positioned vertically about midships, the magazine slotted the shells directly into the gun's breech block. The latter was located behind the crew, and the barrel extended below the floor of the cockpit, with the muzzle protruding from beneath the nose fairing. Two (or four) .303-in machine guns were retained for both strafing and air combat, and all these guns were aimed through one reflector sight – the firing buttons were positioned on the control column. The Molins gun had a muzzle velocity of 2950 ft per second, and the ideal range from which to open fire was 1800-1500 yards.

'Tsetse' operations began on 24 October 1943 with a patrol by two Mk XVIIIs flown by Sqn Ldr C Rose DFC, DFM and Sgt Cowley, and Flg Off A Bonnett, RCAF, and Plt Off Mc D 'Pickles' McNicol. The former crew was lost on 4 November when they crashed into the sea during an attack on a trawler in the Bay of Biscay. Rose fired two shells, but was either hit by return fire or by a ricochet from one of his own rounds.

The mine-swept channels off the French Atlantic coast which led to U-boat bases at Brest, Lorient, St Nazaire, La Rochelle and Bordeaux were the ideal 'killing grounds' because the water depth was too shallow to permit the U-boats to crash-dive if attacked. On 7 November, Al Bonnett scored hits on U-123, which was returning on the surface to Brest. After the first dive, Bonnett's cannon jammed, so he strafed the U-boat with

HJ732/G (G denoted that the aircraft was secret and had to be guarded at all times), which served as the prototype FB XVIII 'Tsetse', had initially been built as an FB VI Series I aircraft. Note the muzzle of the 'six pounder' 57 mm Molins gun protruding from beneath the quartet of Browning .303-in machine guns, which were later halved in number in an effort to save weight, and thus allow more fuel to be carried. 'Tsetses' operated exclusively with No 618 Sqn (Special Detachment) on anti-submarine, ground attack and anti-shipping strikes during 1943-44

machine gun fire. Attacking in a Mk XVIII required a dive from about 5000 ft at a 30° angle, with the turn-and-bank indicator dead central – the slightest drift would cause the gun to jam. As a result of this attack, escort vessels were now provided for the U-boats.

By 1 January 1944, No 248 Sqn's Mosquito Conversion Flight had 16 'Tsetses' and four FB VIs on strength, and on 16 February the unit moved to Portreath. It flew its first first interceptor and anti-shipping patrols into the Bay of Biscay just four days later.

On 10 March four FB VIs which had escorted two Mk XVIIIs to an area about 30 miles north of Gijon, on the Spanish coast, tangled with about ten Ju 88s that had been sent to cover a convoy comprising four destroyers and a U-boat. Two Ju 88s were downed by the FB VIs while the 'Tsetses' attacked the convoy. Sqn Ldr Phillips carried out four attacks on the U-boat and Flg Off Turner two. They damaged a destroyer and Phillips downed a Ju 88 with four shells from his Molins gun.

On 25 March, whilst patrolling in the Il de Yen area of the Bay of Biscay, two 'Tsetses' (MM425/L, flown by Flg Offs Doug Turner and Des Curtis, and HX903/I, crewed by Flg Off A H Hilliard and Wt Off J Hoyle) sank U-976, which was returning to St Nazaire with a destroyer and two minesweepers after being recalled from her second war cruise. Flak from the escorts, which were attacked by the four FB VIs of No 248 Sqn (led by Flt Lt L S Dobson) was intense. Turner made four attacks on U-976 and Hilliard one before the vessel submerged, leaving a patch of oil 100 yards long by 30 yards wide on the surface. The survivors were picked up by escorting minesweepers.

Two days later, in the same area, these two 'Tsetse' crews, escorted by six FB VIs of No 248 Sqn (led by Flt Lt J H B Rollett), made attacks on U-769 and U-960, which were en route to La Pallice. A heavy flak barrage was put up by the U-boats' escort of four 'M' Class minesweepers and two *Sperrbrechers* (merchantmen converted to flak ships). Hilliard's Mosquito was hit in the nose by a 37 mm shell, but fortunately the armour plating beneath the instrument panel cushioned the impact and the crew reached Portreath safely – Flt Sgt L A Compton (in LR363/X) crash-landed on his return. U-960, which was badly damaged in the attack, limped into La Pallice for repairs. A year later she was sunk in the Mediterranean through a combination of US destroyers, Wellingtons and a Ventura.

On 11 April a 'Tsetse' piloted by Flt Lt B C Roberts attacked a U-boat off St Nazaire while nine FB VIs of Nos 248 and 151 Sqns dealt with her four-ship escort, and a dozen Ju 88s. Roberts saw spouts of water near the hull as he fired his Molins, but could claim no definite hits. Flak was again heavy and two FB VIs were downed, but two Ju 88s were claimed destroyed. A third Mosquito was lost in a crash-landing at Portreath.

In May the 'Tsetses' began attacking surface vessels in addition to U-boats, using armour-piercing shells to penetrate the wooden deck-planking of the ships in unison with rocket-firing Beaufighters that struck in shallow dives from 500 ft. On D-Day No 248 Sqn flew anti-shipping, escort and blockading sorties off the Normandy, Brittany and Biscay coasts.

On 7 June two 'Tsetses', flown by Flg Offs Doug Turner DFC and Des Curtis DFC, and Flg Offs Al Bonnett, RCAF, and 'Pickles' McNicol, each made a run on a surfacing U-boat. Twelve 57 mm shells were fired at U-212, but on Bonnett's second run his cannon jammed, which forced him to make a series of dummy dives on the U-boat – the latter crash-dived, leaving a pool of oil and a crewman on the surface. U-212 limped into St Nazaire and was repaired, but was then promptly sunk in July by Royal Navy frigates. Turner's Mosquito was hit by flak in the port wing and engine nacelle, but he and Bonnett made it back to Cornwall.

Bonnett and McNicol were killed on 9 June when Wg Cdr Tony Phillips DSO, DFC (now OC of No 248 Sqn) collided with their Mosquito whilst coming into land following a search for survivors from a German destroyer in the Channel. Phillips lost six feet of his outer wing but landed safely – he and his navigator, Flg Off R W 'Tommy' Thomson DFC, were killed on 4 July during an attack off the Brest Peninsular.

On 10 June, four No 248 Sqn Mosquitoes (led by Flt Lt S G Nunn and Flg Off J M Carlin in LR347/T) attacked U-821 with such force off Ushant that the crew abandoned ship – the U-boat was sunk by a Liberator from No 206 Sqn. That afternoon, No 248 Sqn's Flt Lt E H Jeffreys DFC and Flg Off D A Burden were downed by a motor launch carrying the survivors of U-821during a follow up strike by two 'Tsetses' and four FB VIs. The launch was quickly sunk by the Molins cannons.

During May-June the Norwegians of No 333 Sqn also became involved in attacks on U-boats. On 26 May Lt J M Jacobsen and Sub Lt Humlen (in HR262/N), and Lts Hans Engebrightsen and Odd Jonassen, (in HP904/E) damaged U-958 in an attack off Norway – Jonassen was killed in action on 11 June when he and Engebrightsen were accidentally shot down by Spitfires. Three days later Lt Erling Johansen and 2/Lt Lauritz Humlen (in HP864/H) attacked and damaged U-290 again off Norway, putting the boat out of commission until August. On 16 June Johansen and Humlen sighted U-998 on the surface off the Norwegian coast and duly attacked with cannons blazing. Two depth charges were also dropped from 100 ft which so badly damaged the U-boat that it was paid off in Bergen harbour later that month.

On a subsequent patrol that same day, Lt Jacob M Jacobson and 2/Lt Per Hansen sighted and attacked U-804, which was also badly damaged and forced into Bergen for repairs. this vessel would later fall victim to Banff Wing Mosquitoes on 9 April 1945.

On 23 June Flt Sgts Leslie Doughty and R Grime were one of six crews from No 248 Sqn sent to patrol between Ushant and Lorient. However, they became separated from the others in bad light, but this did not stop Doughty flying on and locating a convoy of escorts and U-155, which was about to enter Lorient following her ninth patrol. The crew attacked with cannons and machine guns, and also dropped two depth charges from 50 ft. Doughty's action earned him a promotion to warrant officer and the award of the DFM. U-155 was so badly damaged in the attack that she was out of action until September, when the refurbished U-boat sailed for Norway.

Twenty-four hours earlier, wing-mounted 25-lb Mk XI depth charges and A VIII mines were used for the first time operationally by Mosquitoes. Portreath-based No 235 Sqn also flew their first FB VI sortie at this time, having completed their last Beaufighter operation on 27 June. The FB VIs flew as escort for the Beaufighters, and also intercepted Do 217s which carried Hs 293 glider bombs for attacks on Allied shipping.

MOSQUITO BOMBER AND FIGHTER-BOMBER SQUADRONS

21 (YH)	140 Wing, 2 Group, 2nd TAF	1655 MTU	8 Group (PFF)
464 RAAF (SB)	140 Wing, 2 Group, 2nd TAF	617 (AJ)	5 Group, Bomber Command
487 RNZAF (EG)	140 Wing, 2 Group, 2nd TAF	618 (OP)	No 18 Group, Coastal Command
107 (OM)	138 Wing, 2 Group, 2nd TAF	143 (NE)	Banff Strike Wing*
305 (SM)	138 Wing, 2 Group, 2nd TAF	235 (LA)	Banff Strike Wing*
613 (SY)	138 Wing, 2 Group, 2nd TAF	248 (DM/WR)	Banff Strike Wing*
105 (PFF) (GB)	2 Group/8 Group (PFF) (from 5/43)	333 RNWAF (KK)	Banff Strike Wing*
109 (PFF) (HS)	2 Group/8 Group (PFF) (from 1/6/43)	334 RNWAF (VB)	Banff Strike Wing*
128 (M5)	8 Group (PFF)	404 RCAF (EO)	Banff Strike Wing*
139 (PFF) (XD)	2 Group/8 Group (PFF) (From 5/43)	489 RNZAF (P6)	Banff Strike Wing*
142 (4H)	8 Group (PFF)	45 (OB)	India
162 (CR)	8 Group (PFF)	47 (KU)	India
163	8 Group (PFF)	82 (UX)	India
571 (8K)	8 Group (PFF)	84 (PY)	India
608 (6T/RAO)	8 Group (PFF)	110 (VE)	India
627 (AZ)	8 Group (PFF)/5 Group (from 13/4/44)	211	India
692 (P3)	8 Group (PFF)	1 RAAF (NA)	Borneo
1409 Met Flt (AE)	8 Group (PFF)		(*Formed, 9/44)

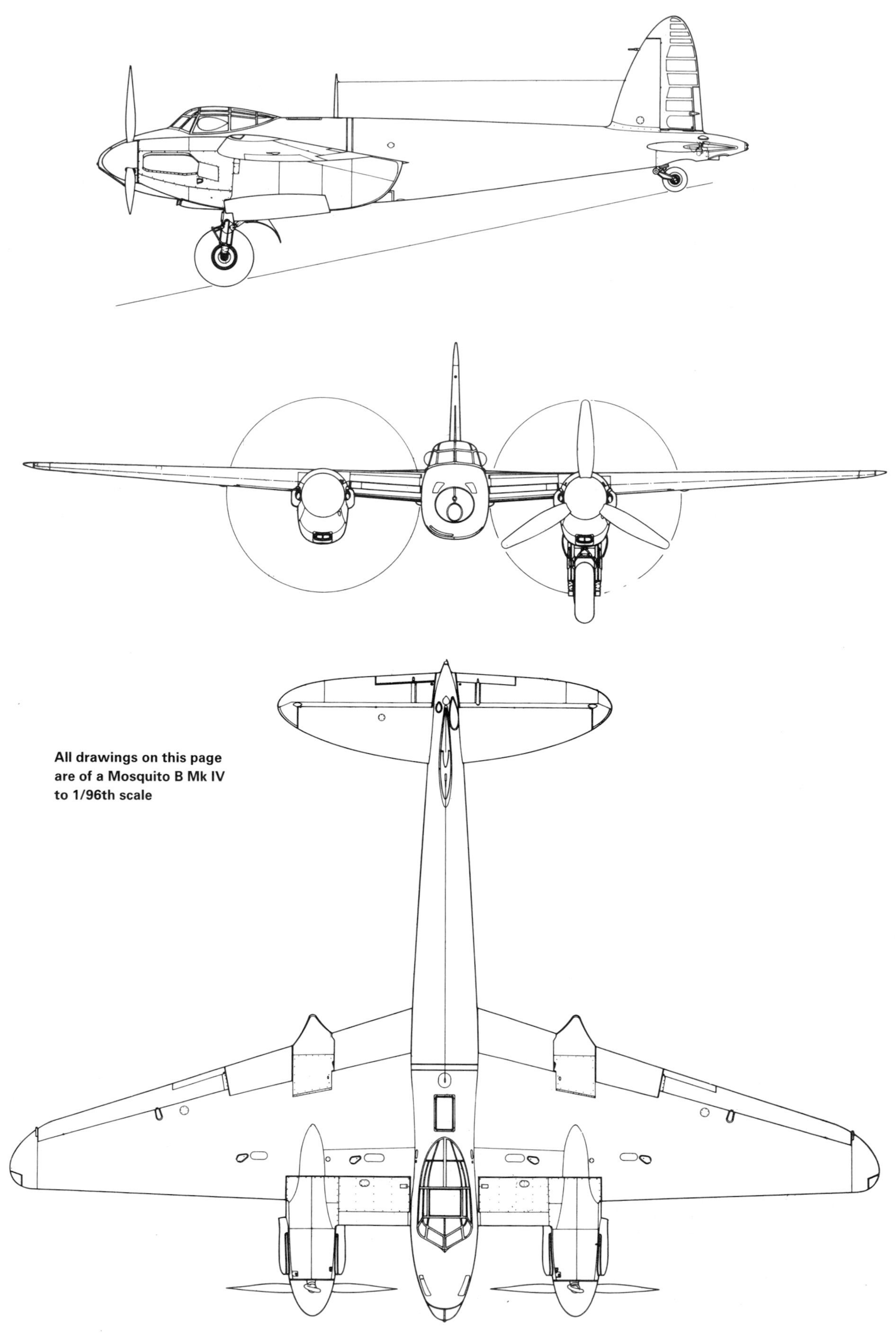

All drawings on this page are of a Mosquito B Mk IV to 1/96th scale

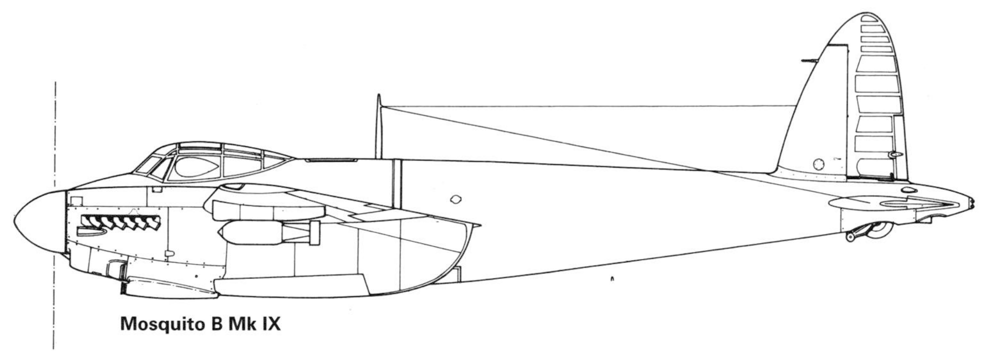

Mosquito B Mk IX

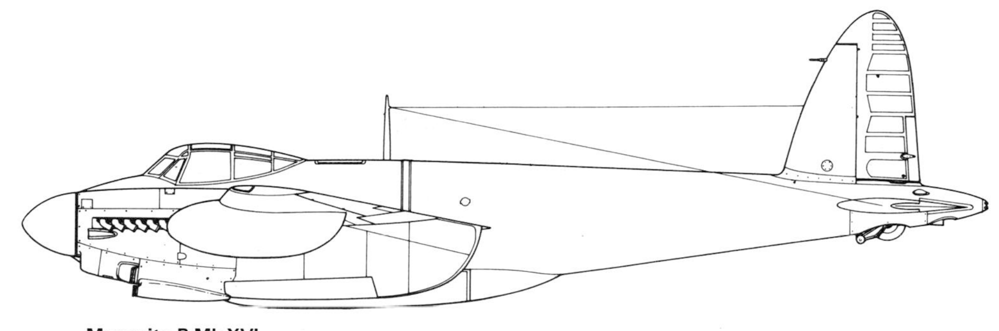

Mosquito B Mk XVI

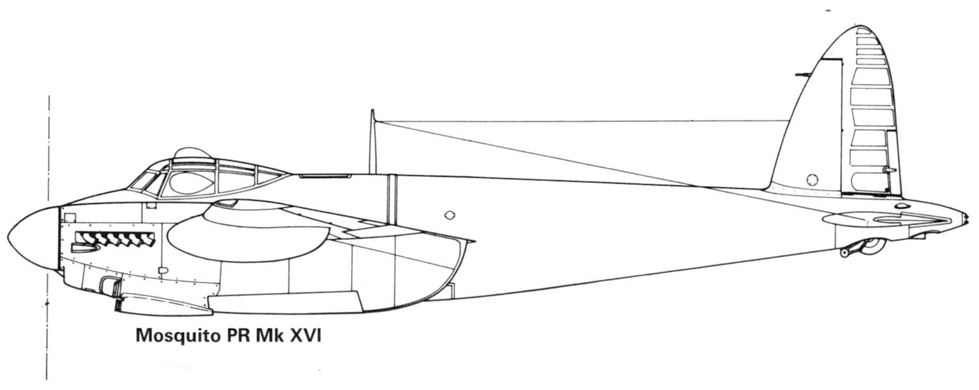

Mosquito PR Mk XVI

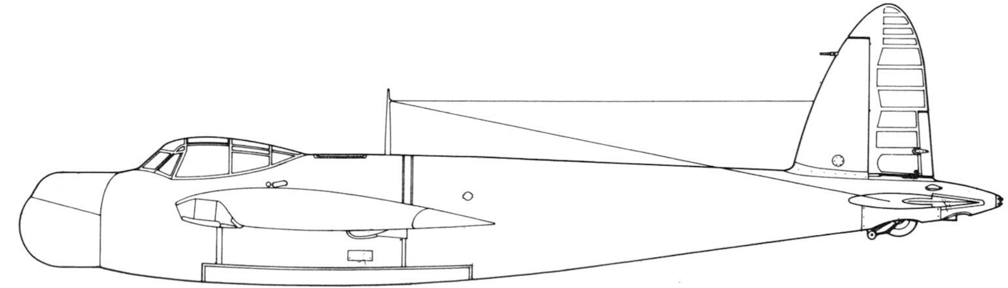

Mosquito B Mk XVI
(radar nose)